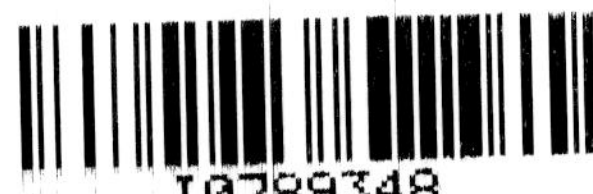

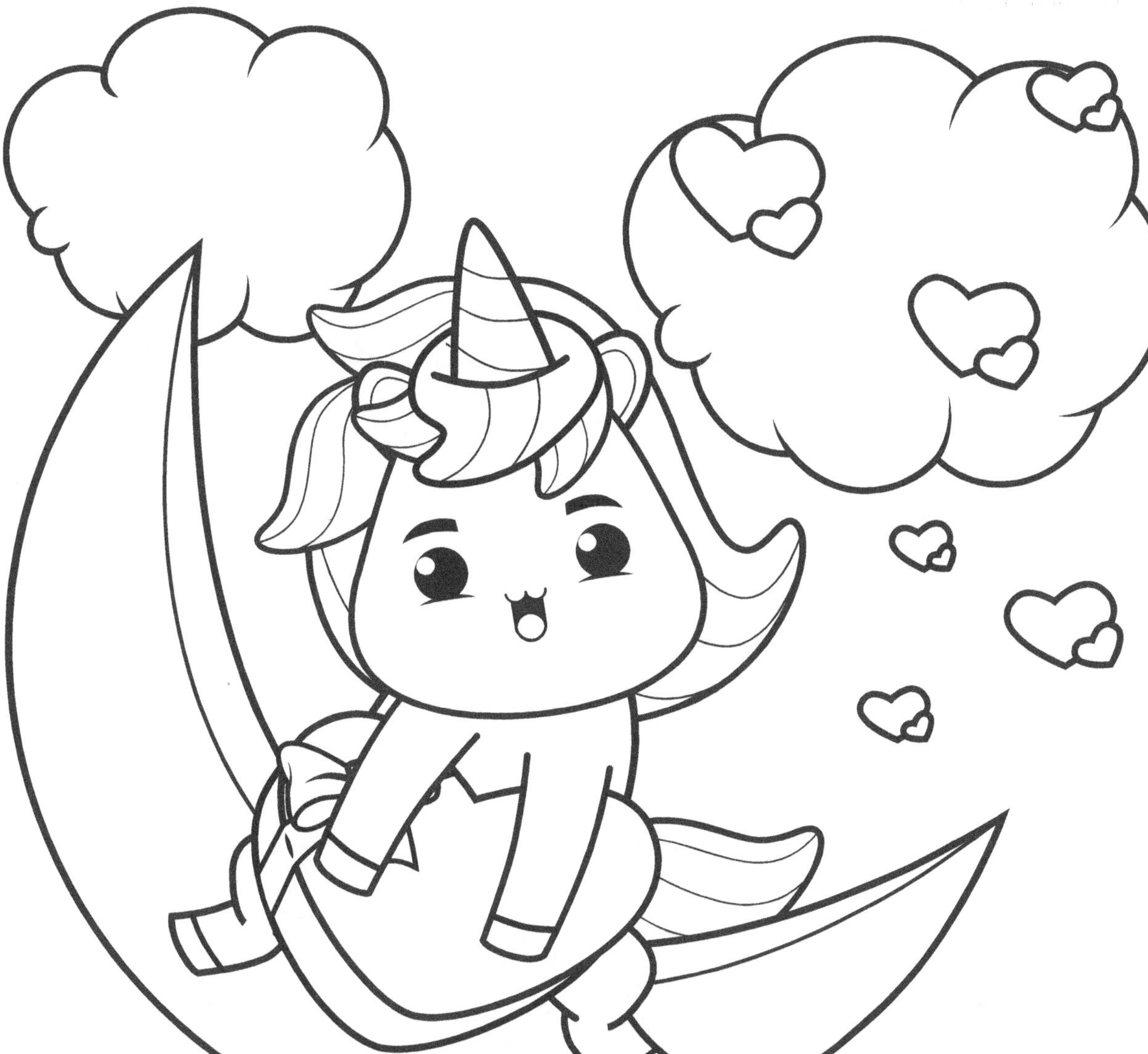

THIS BOOK BELONGS TO

____

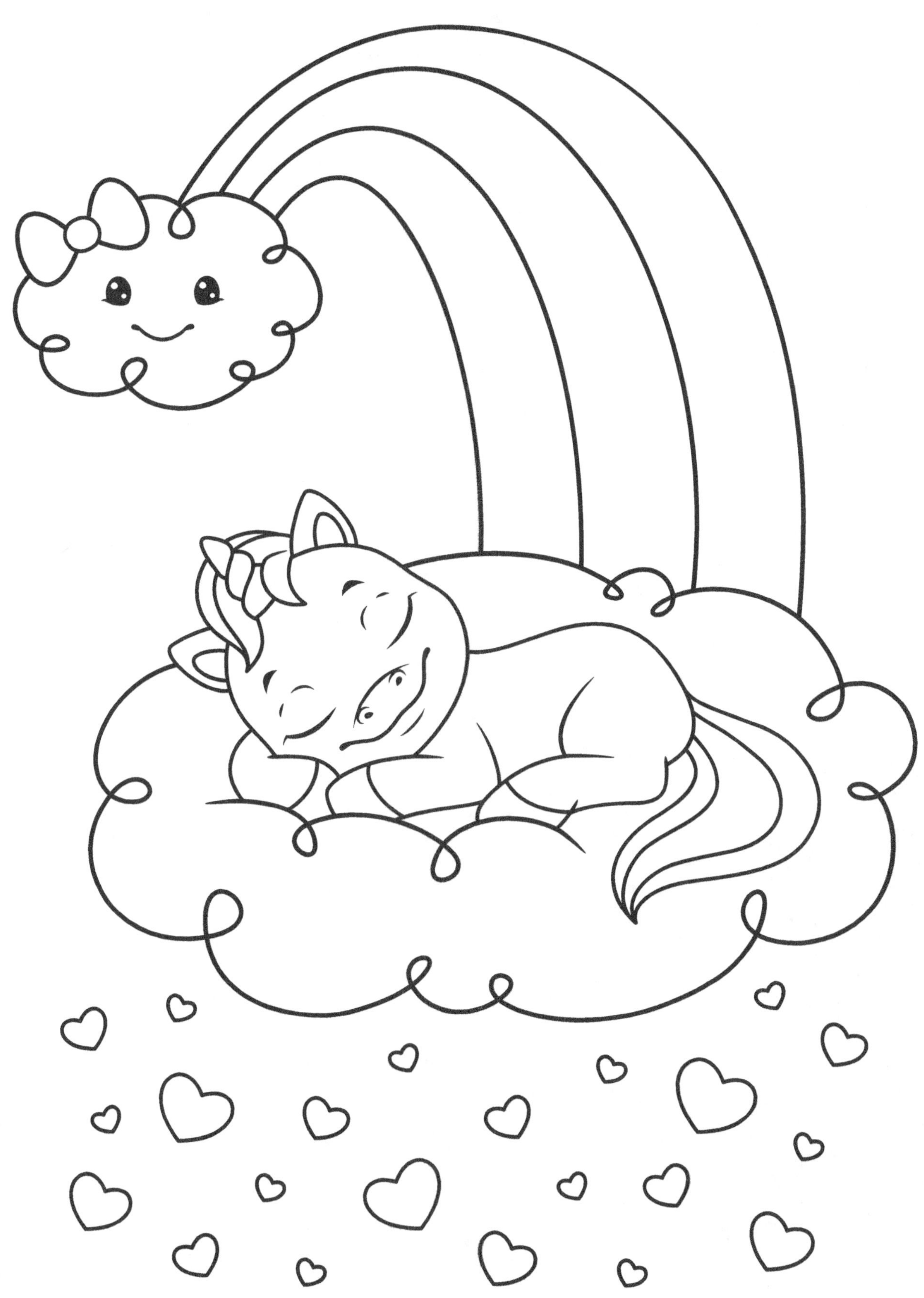

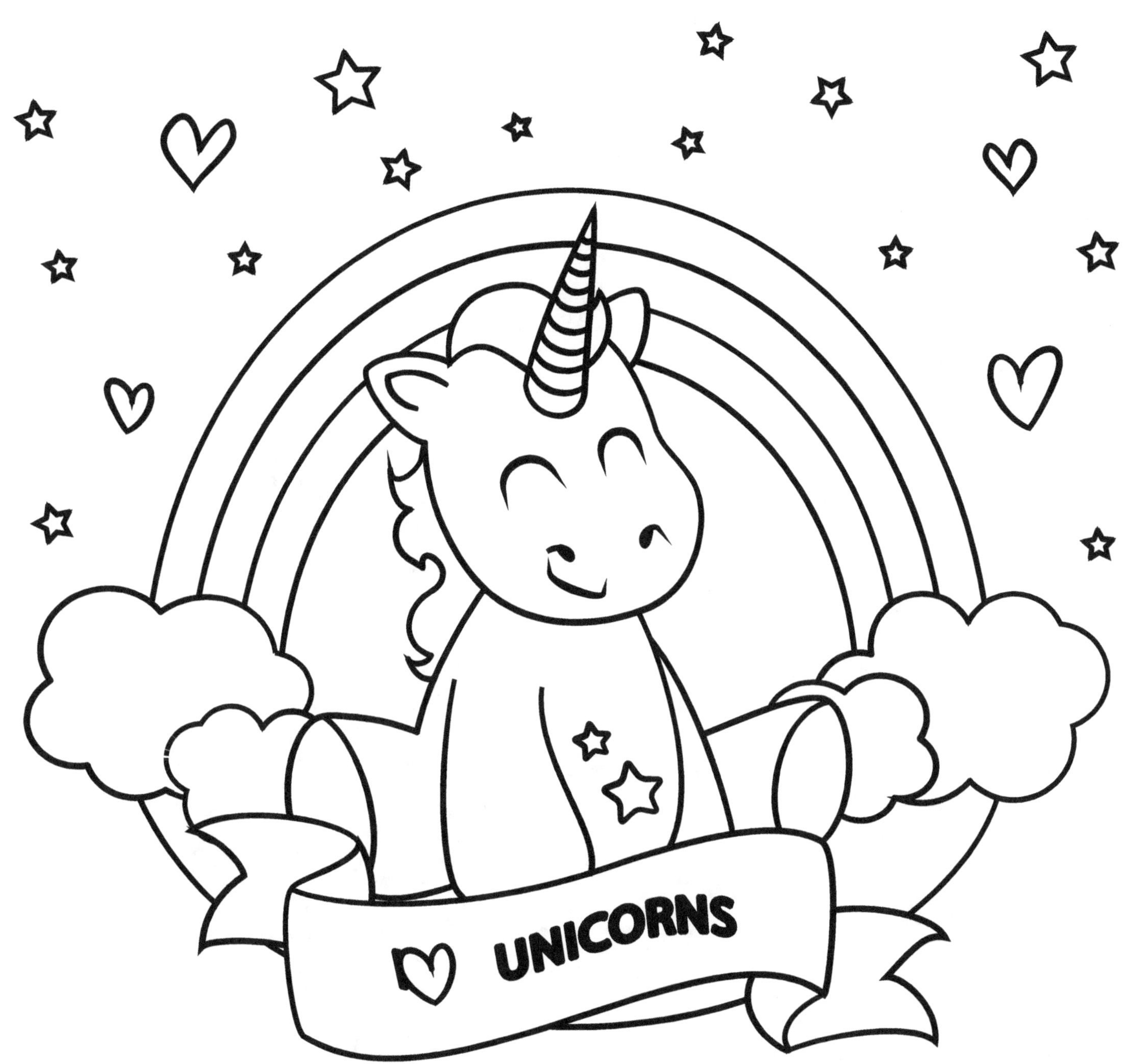
UNICORNS

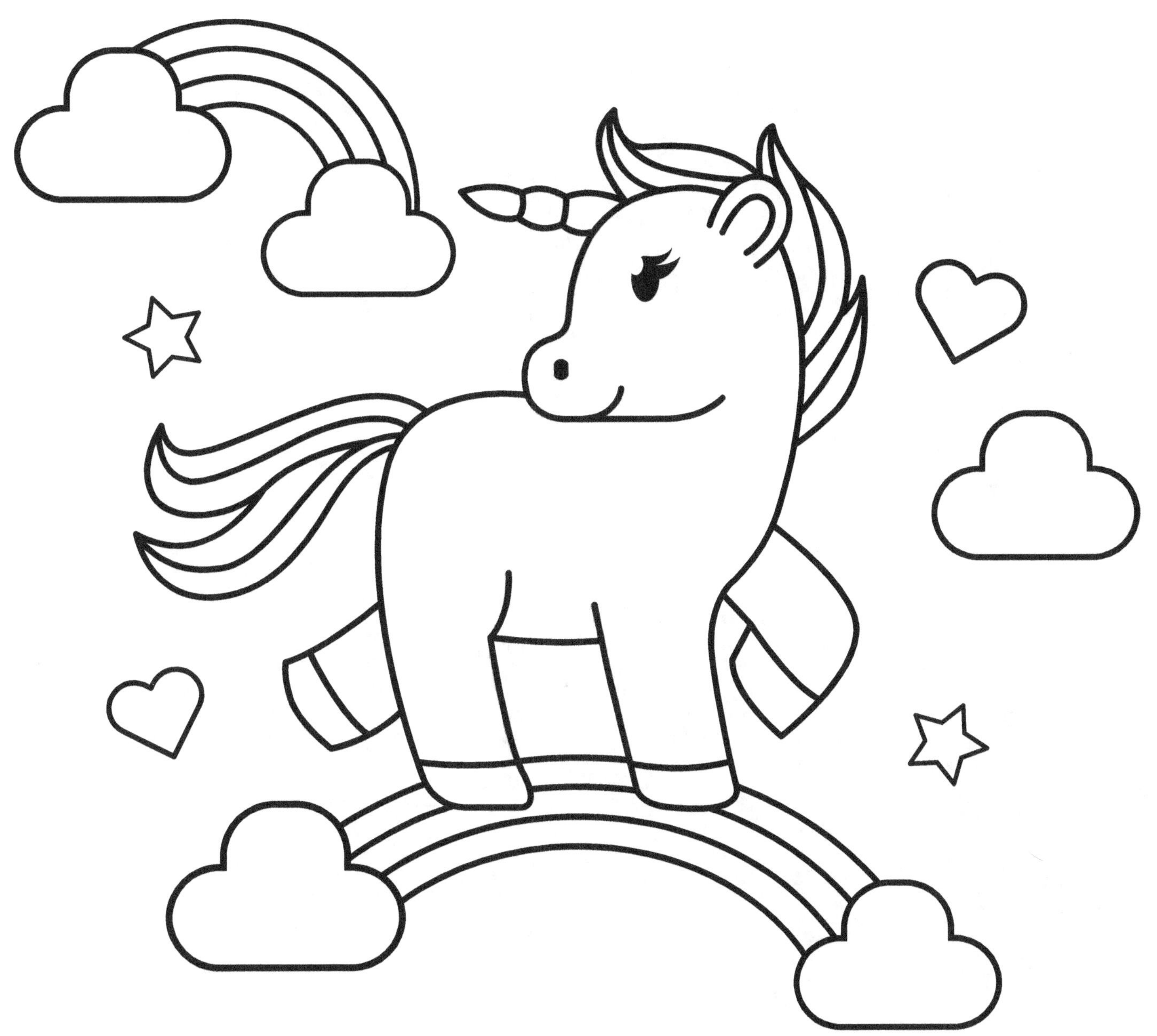

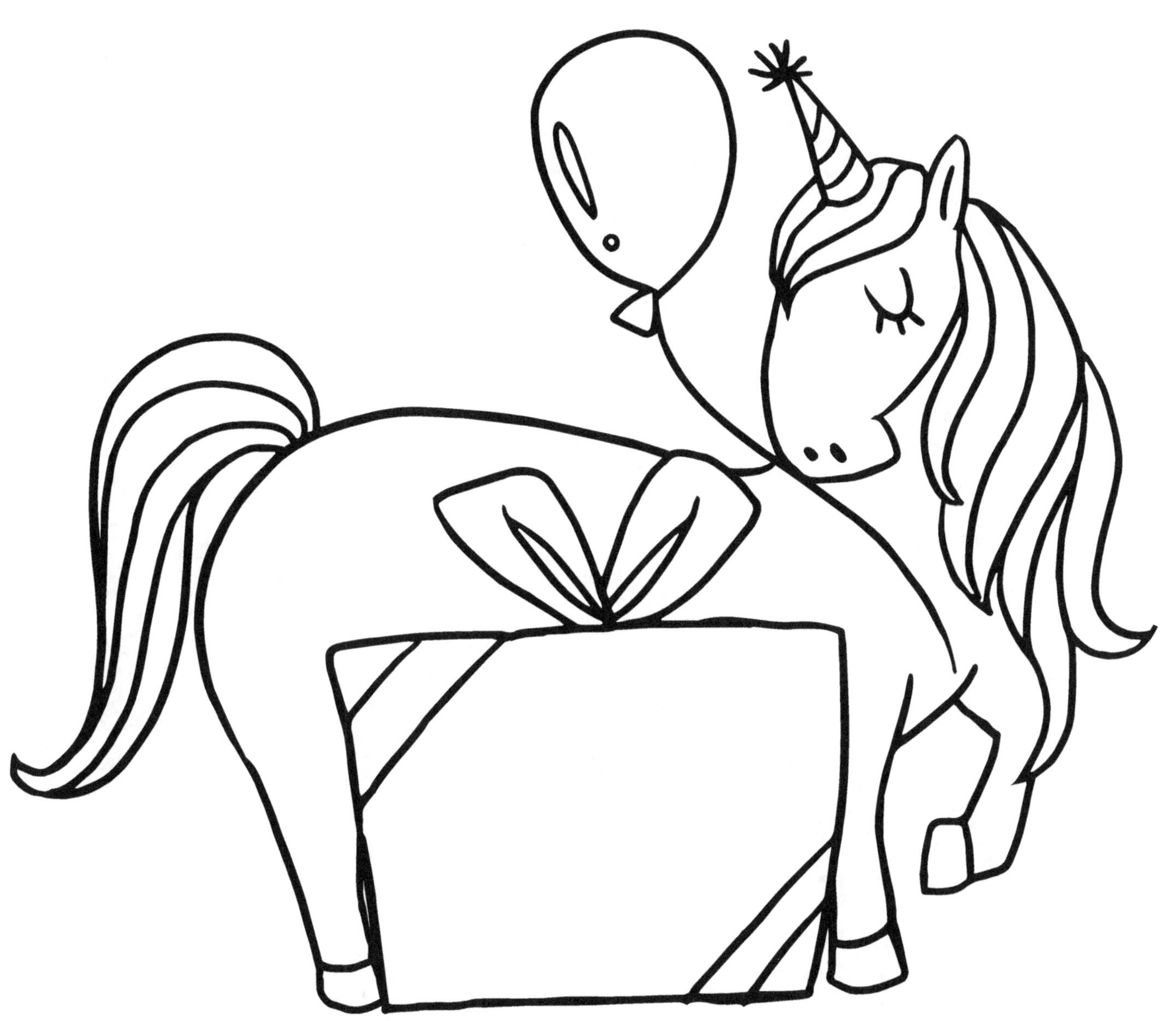

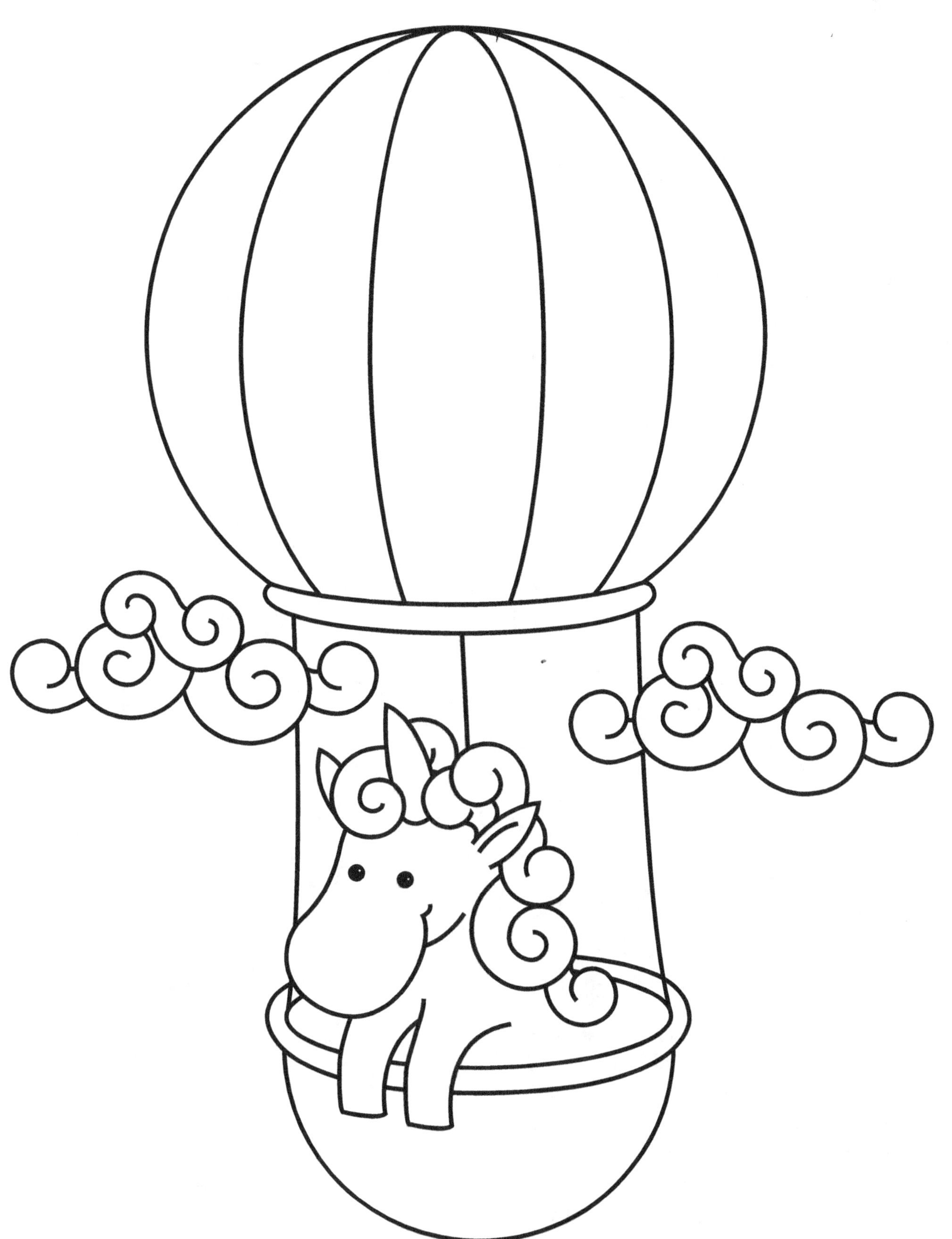

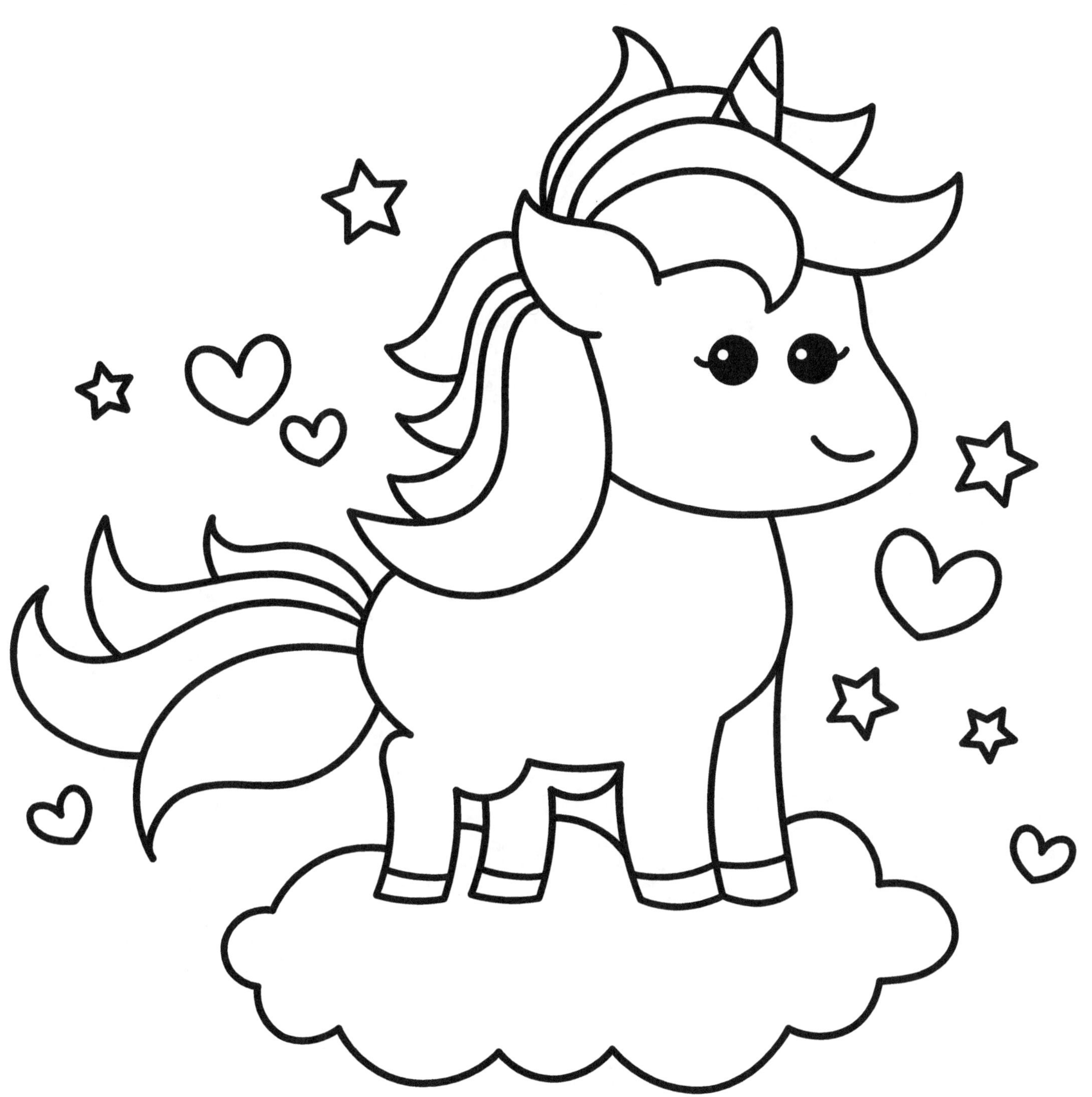

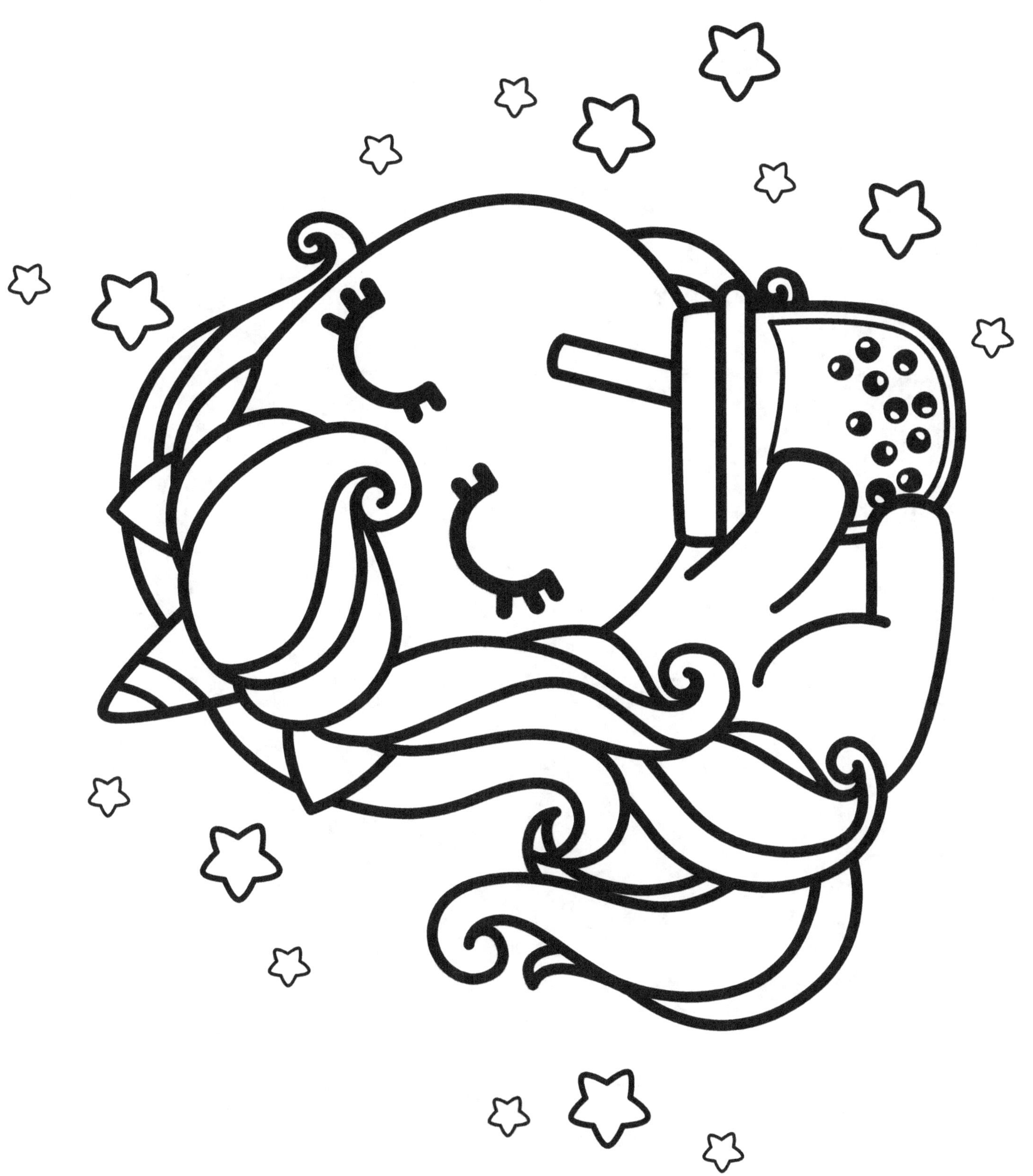

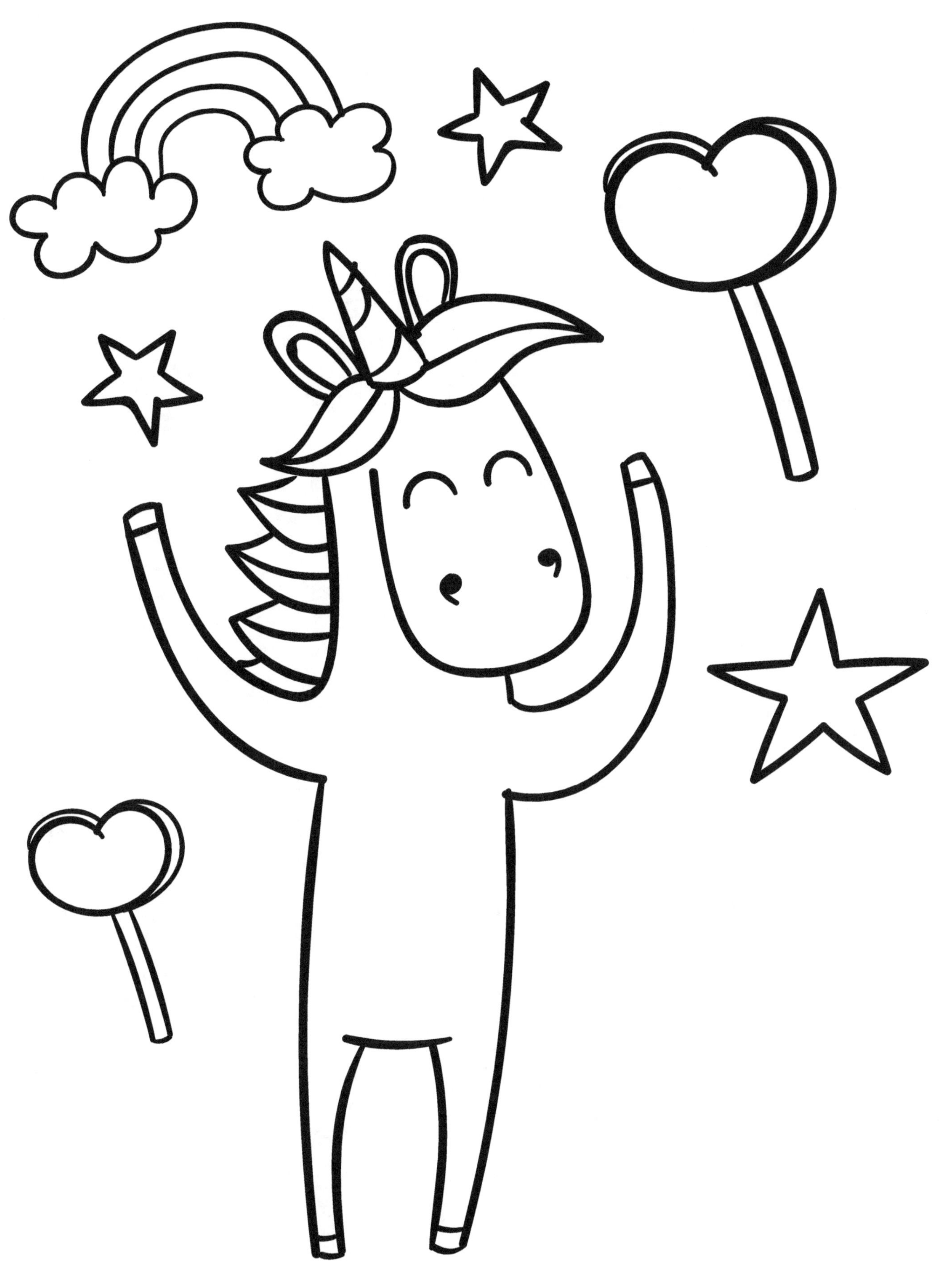

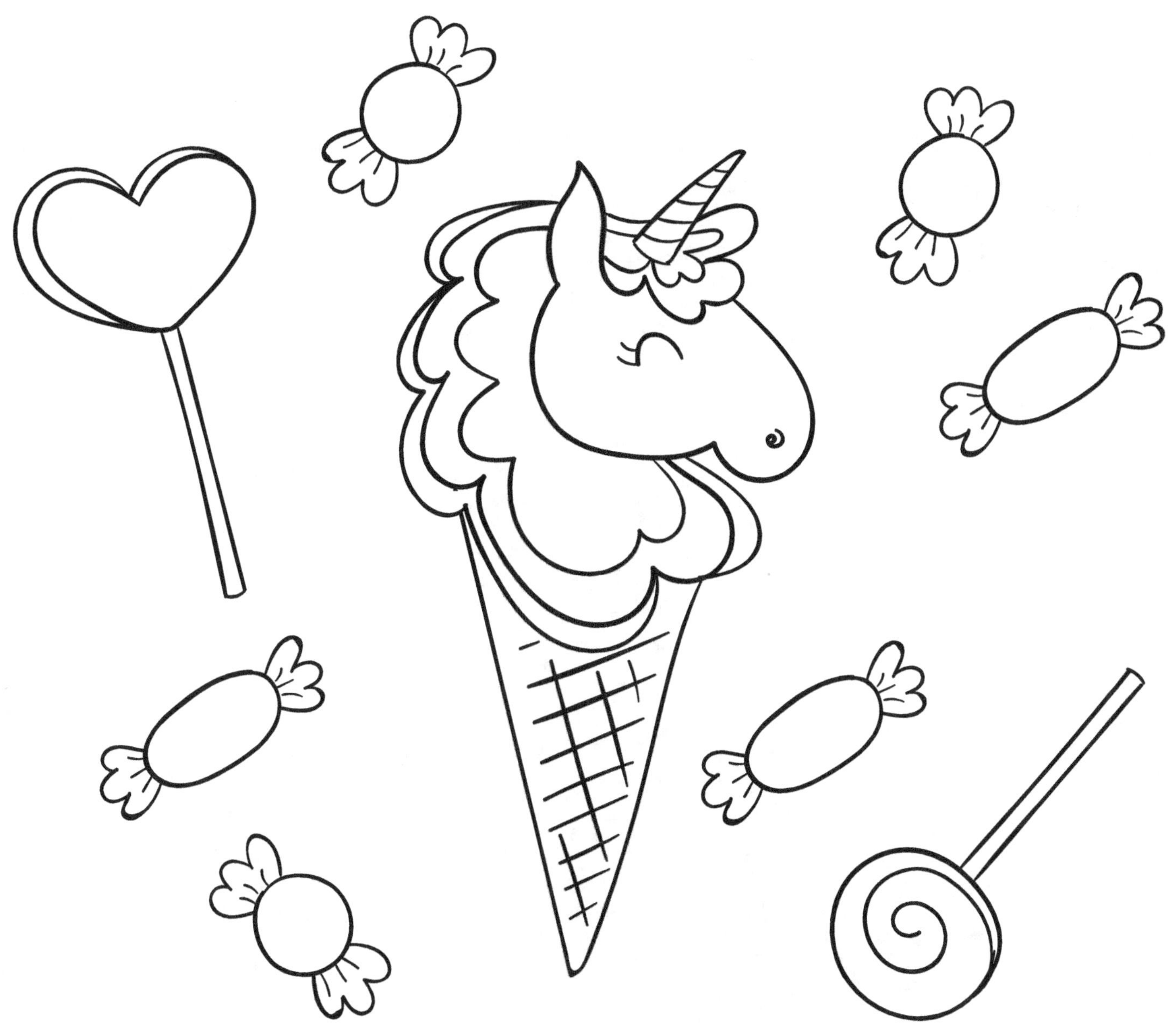

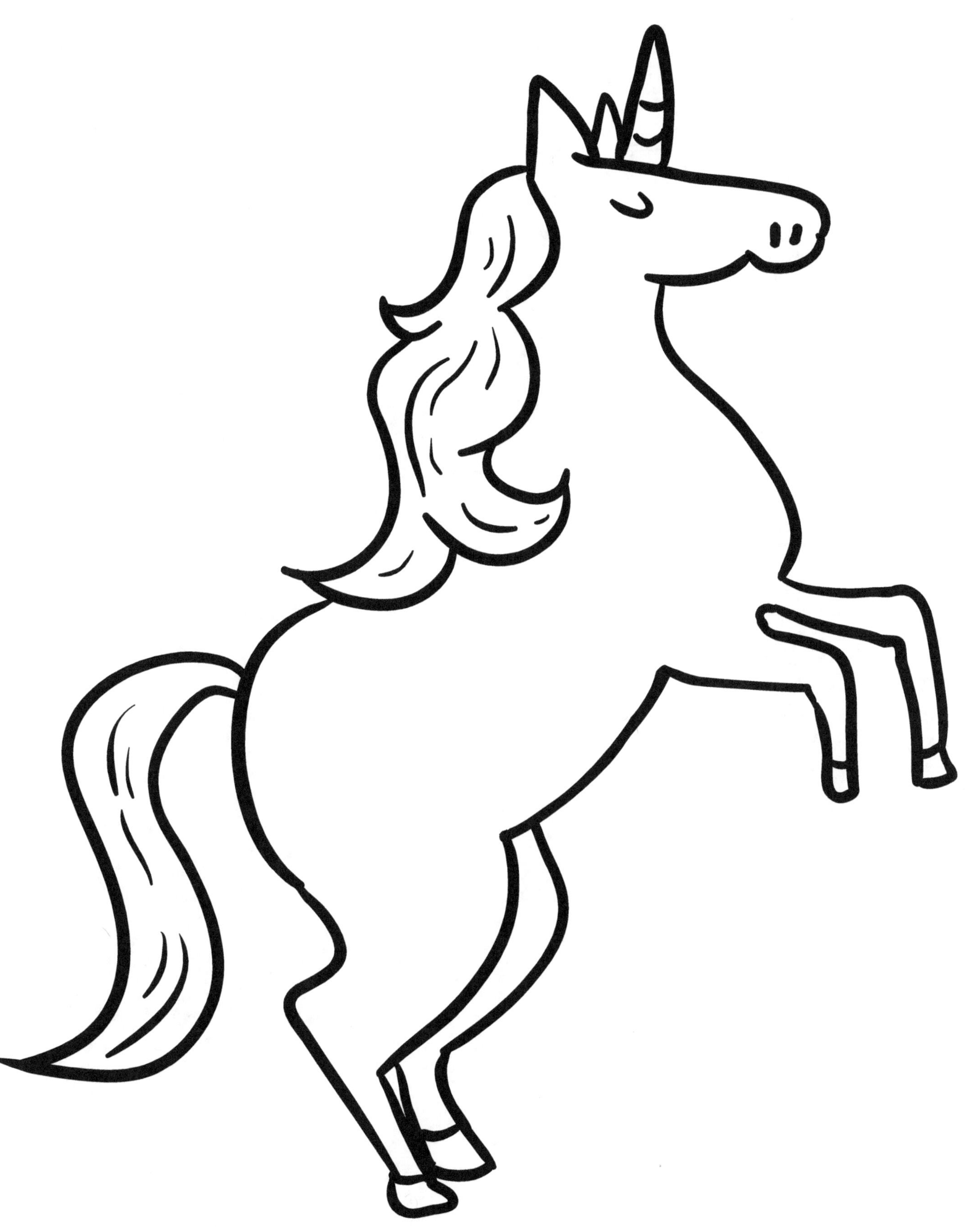

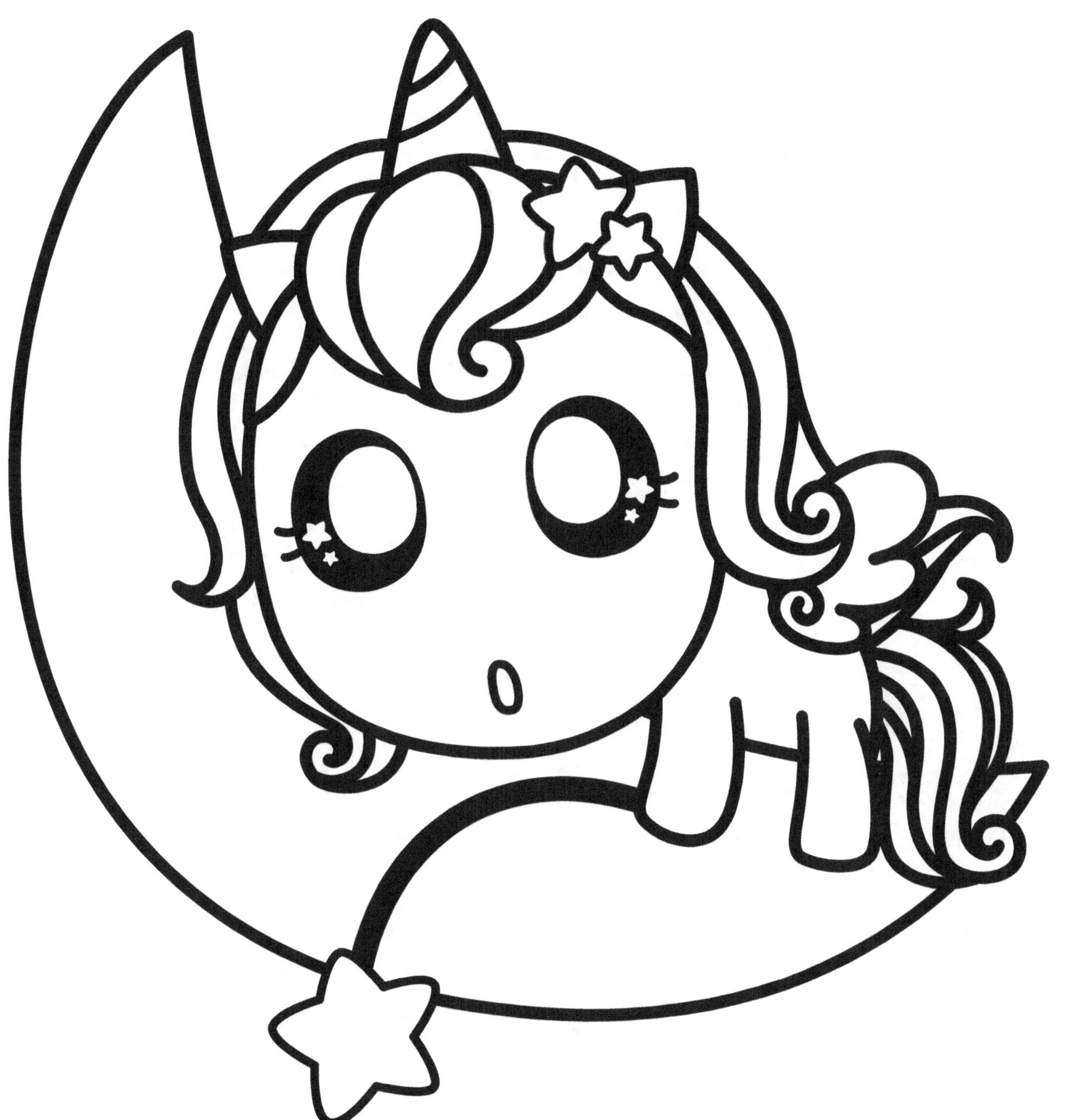

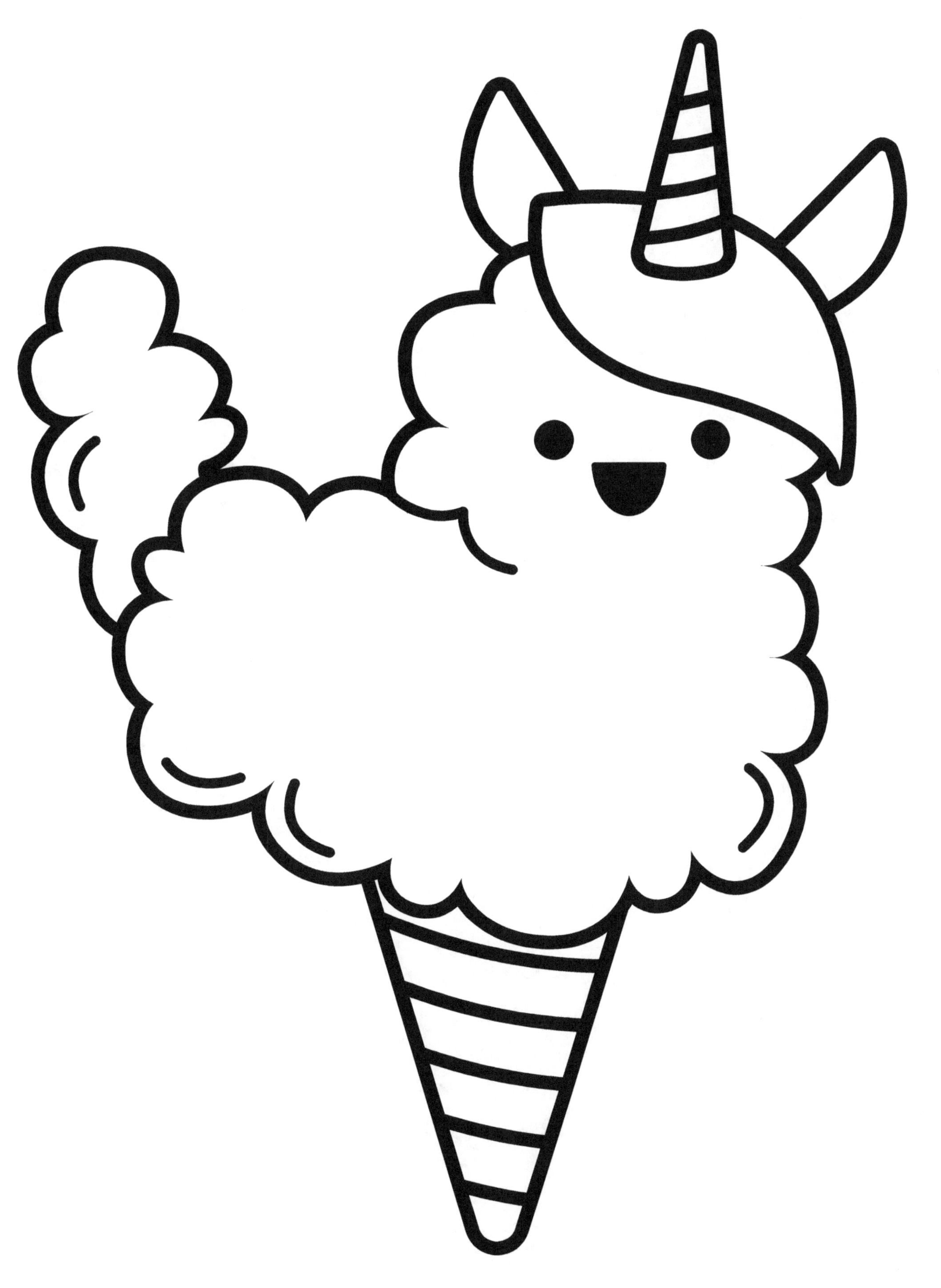

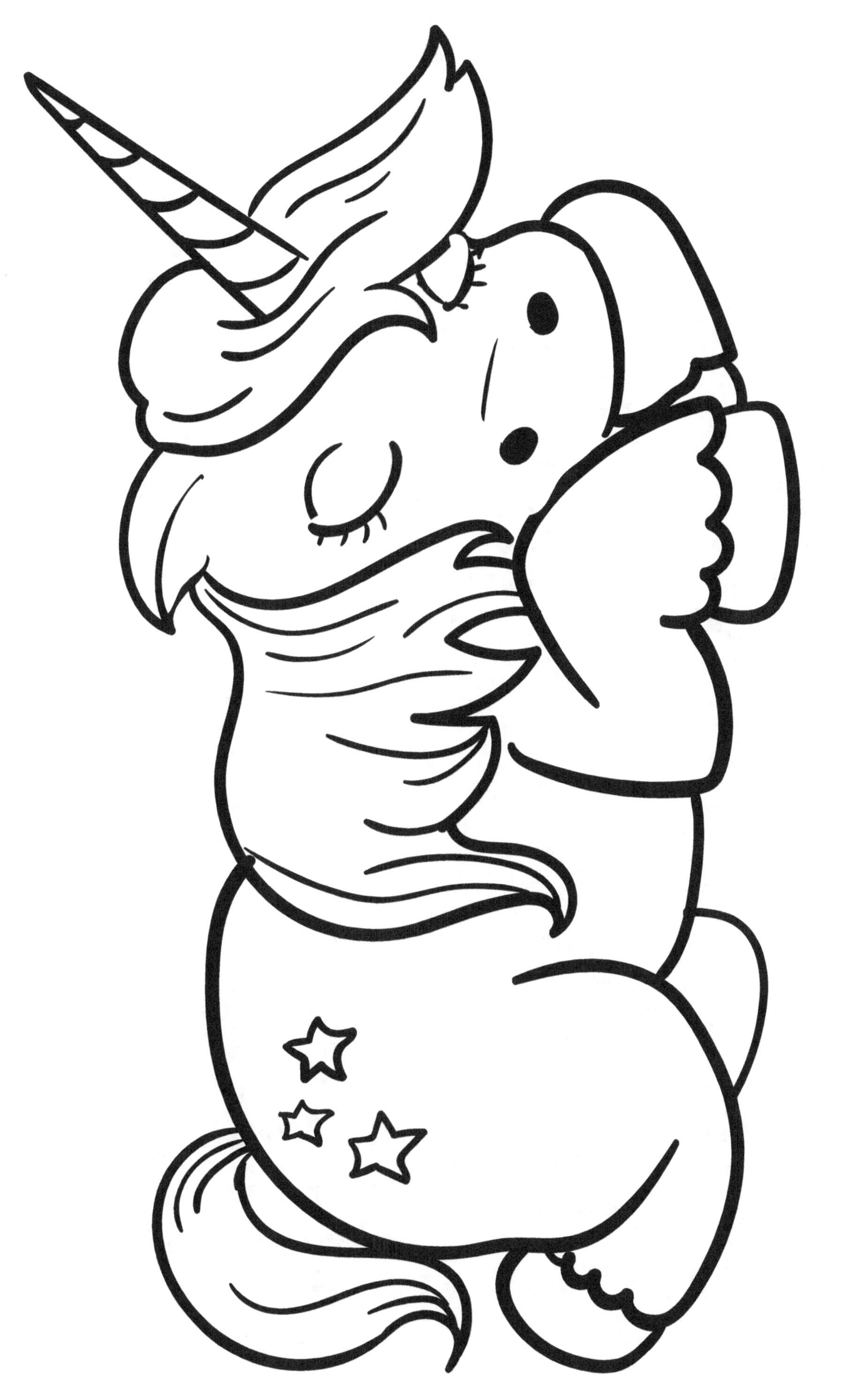

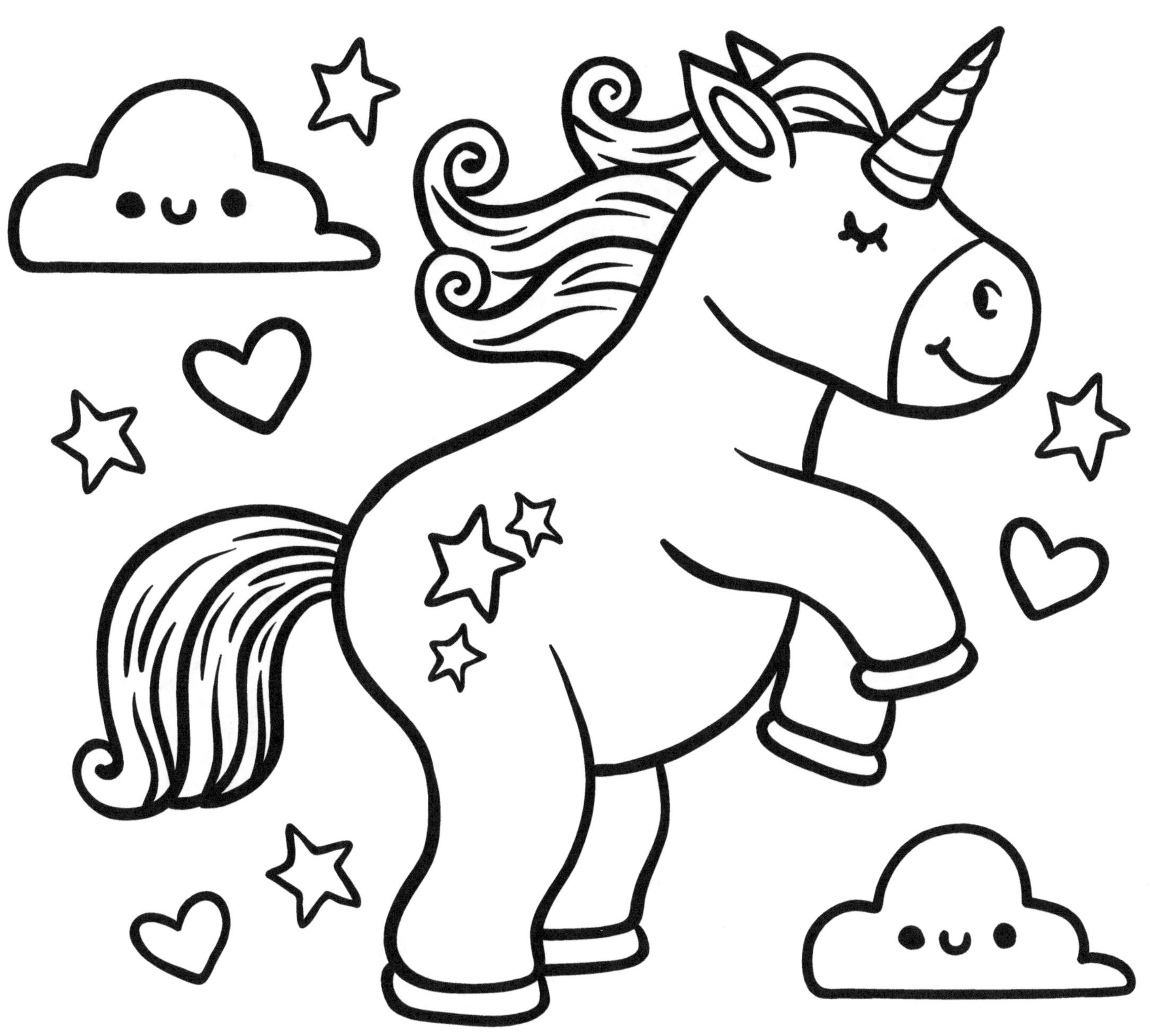

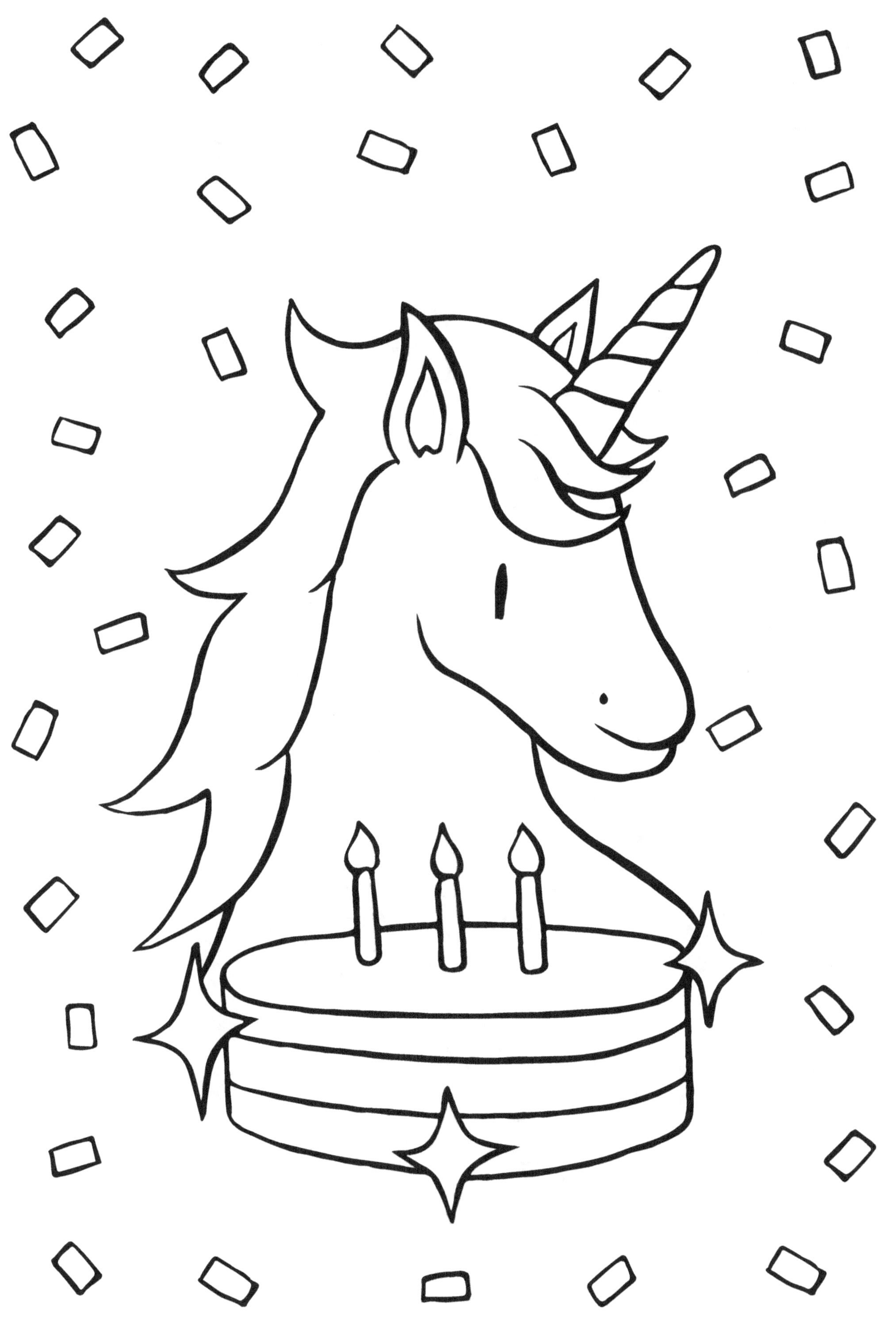

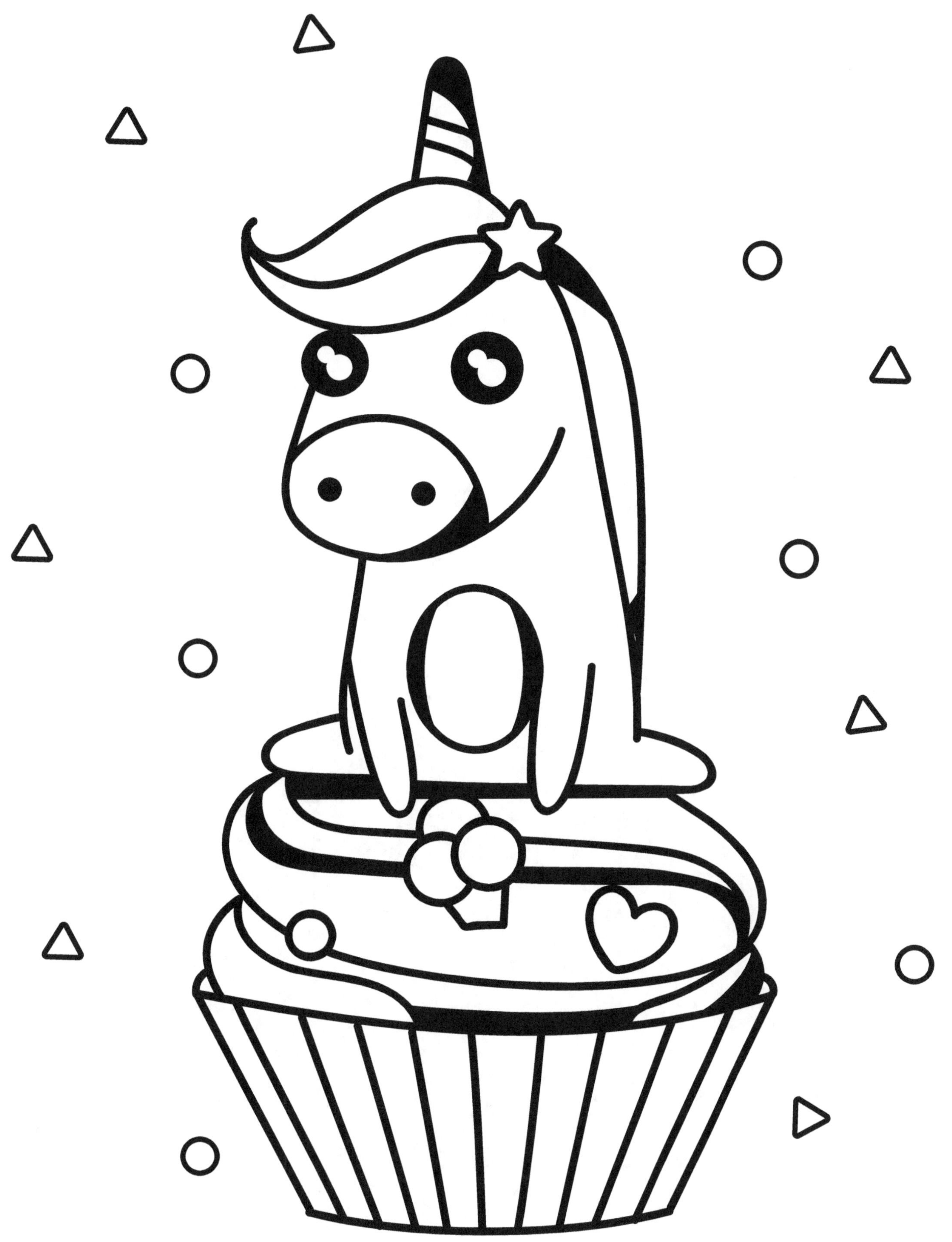

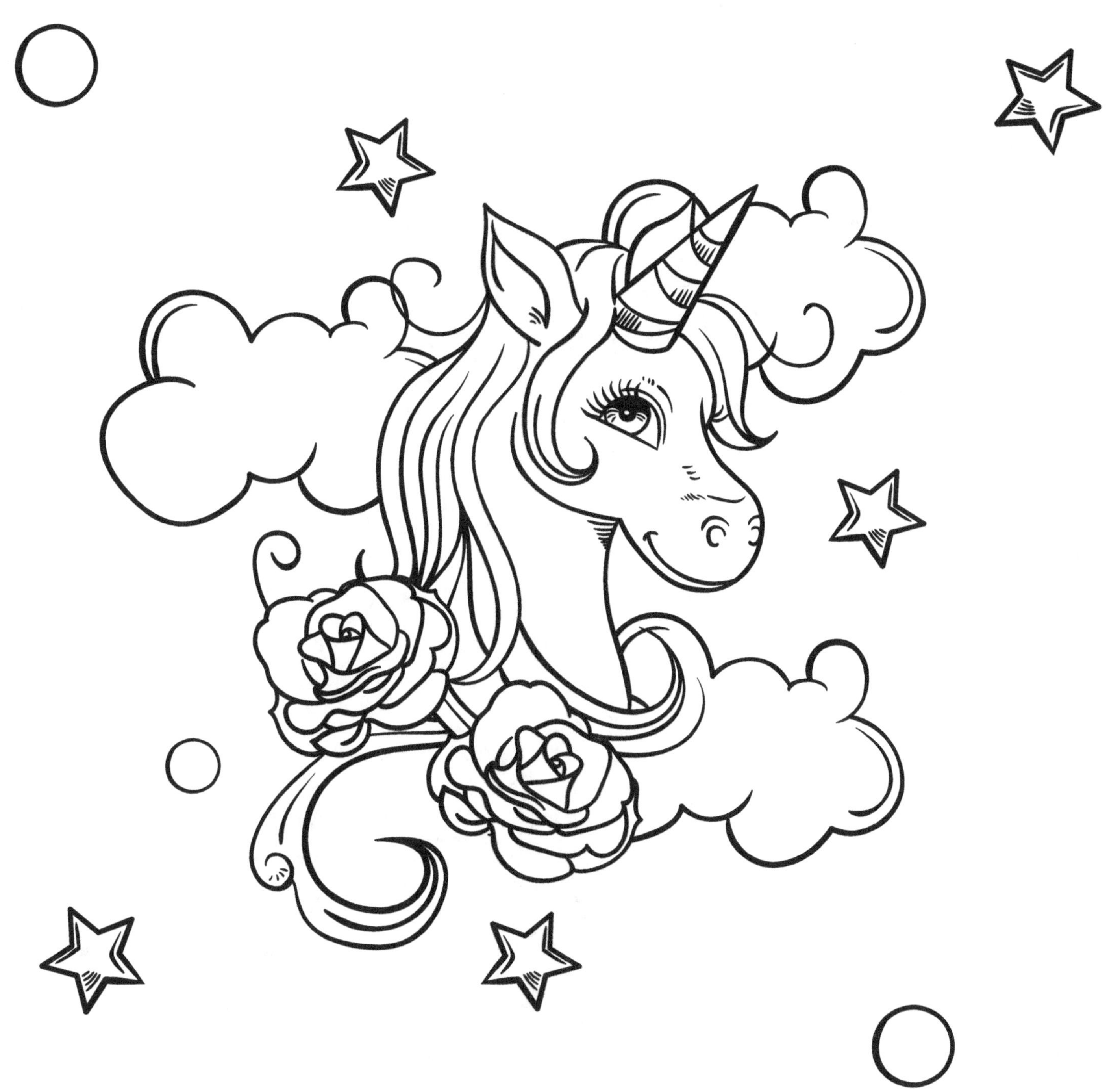

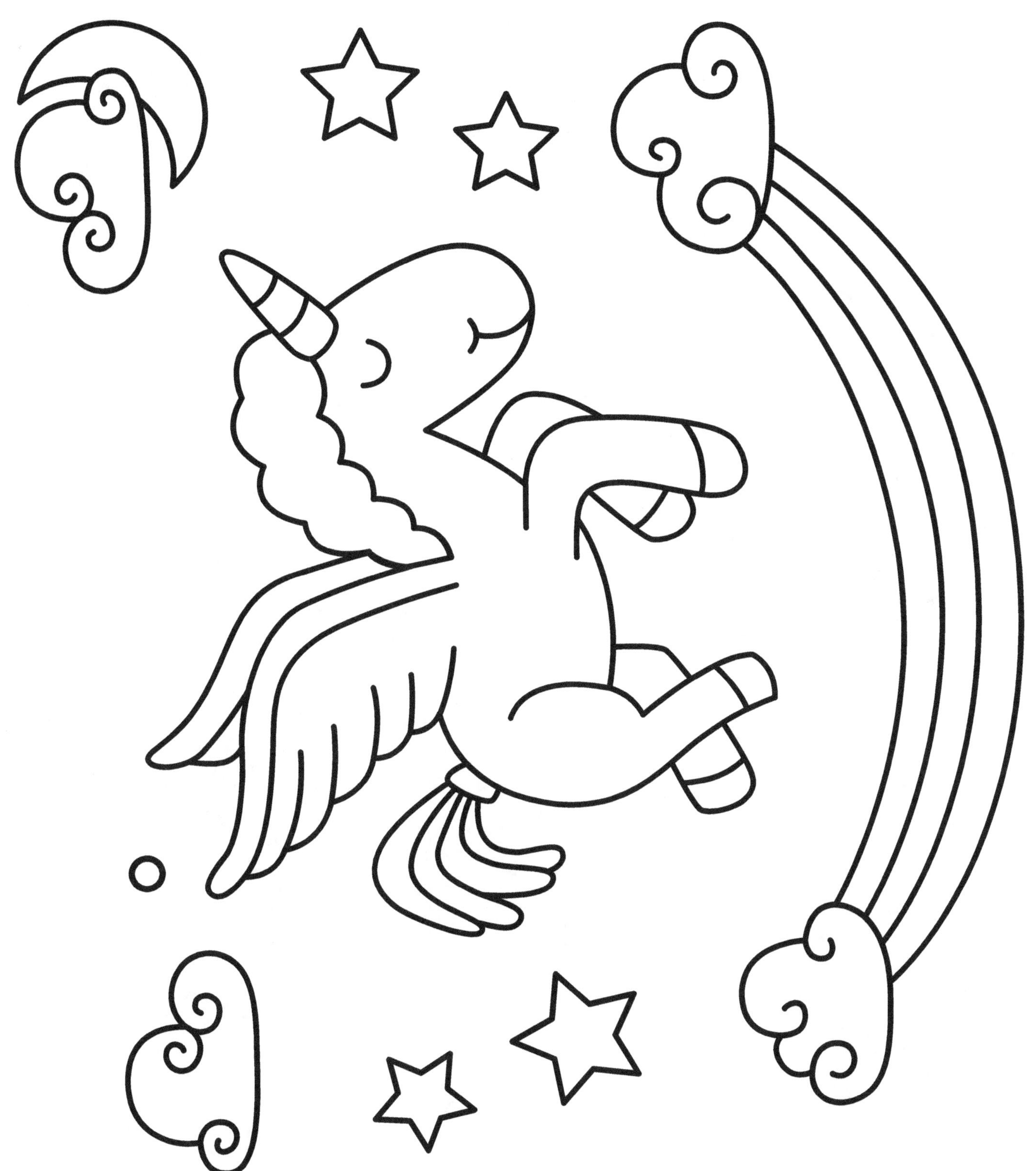

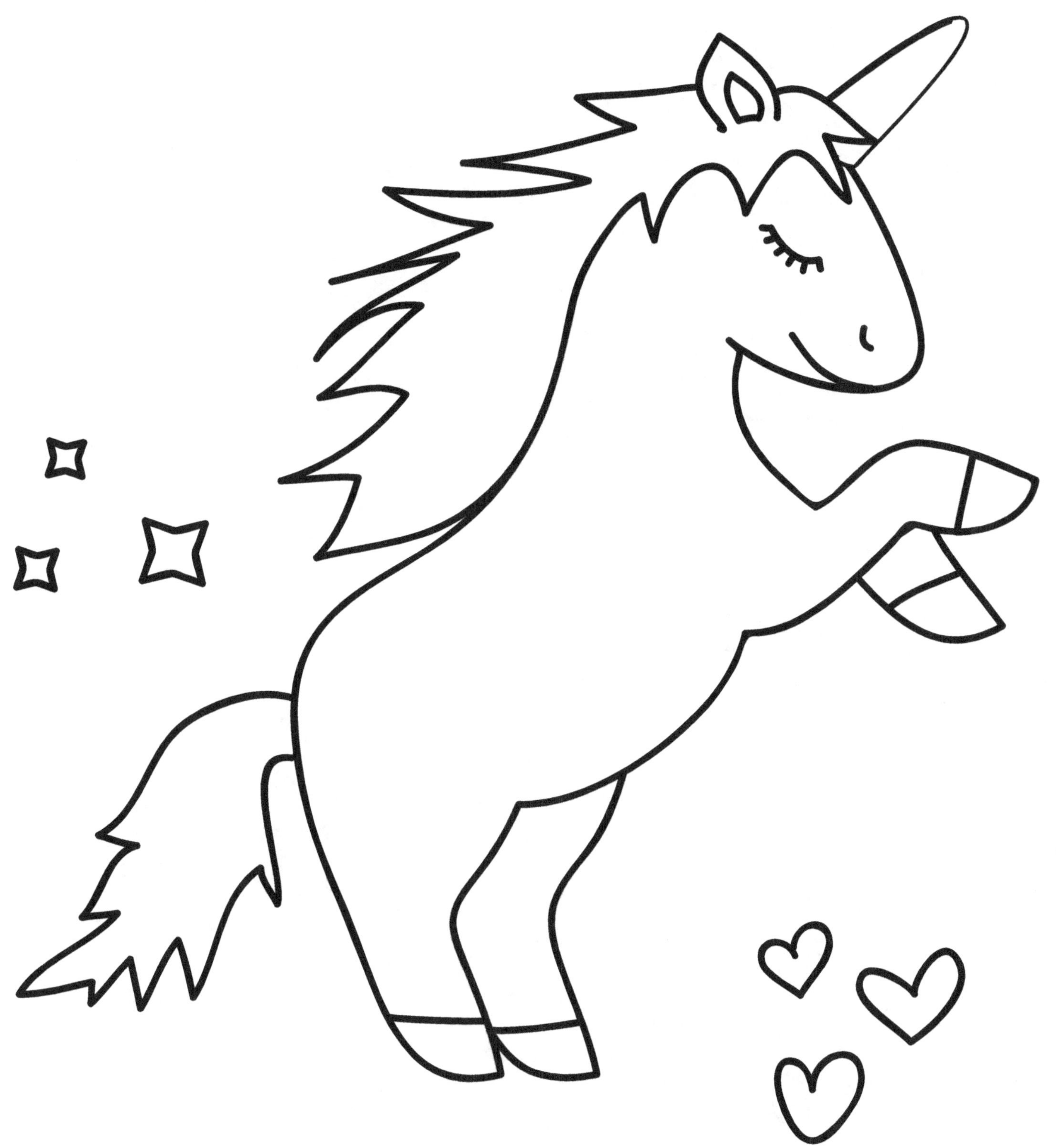

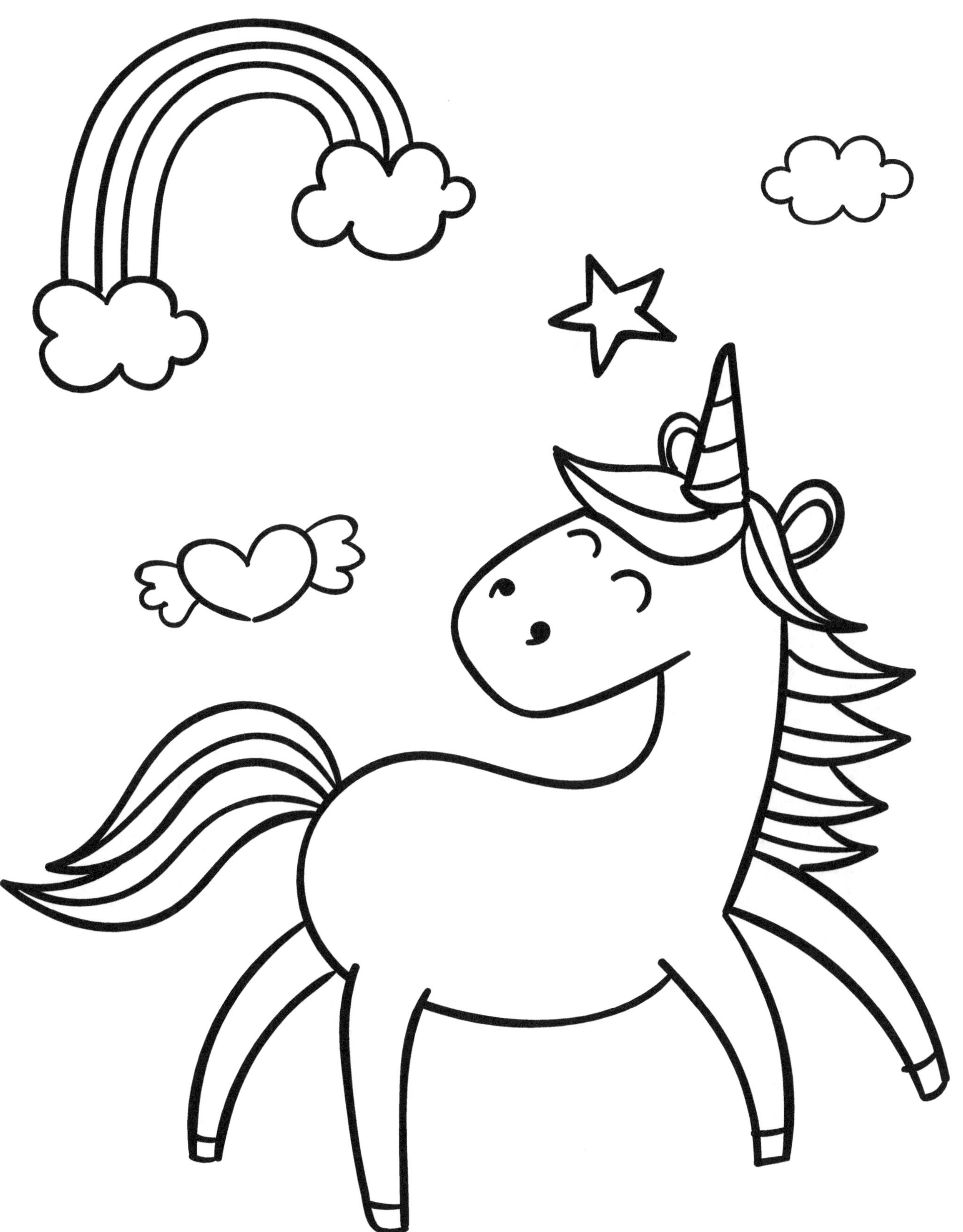

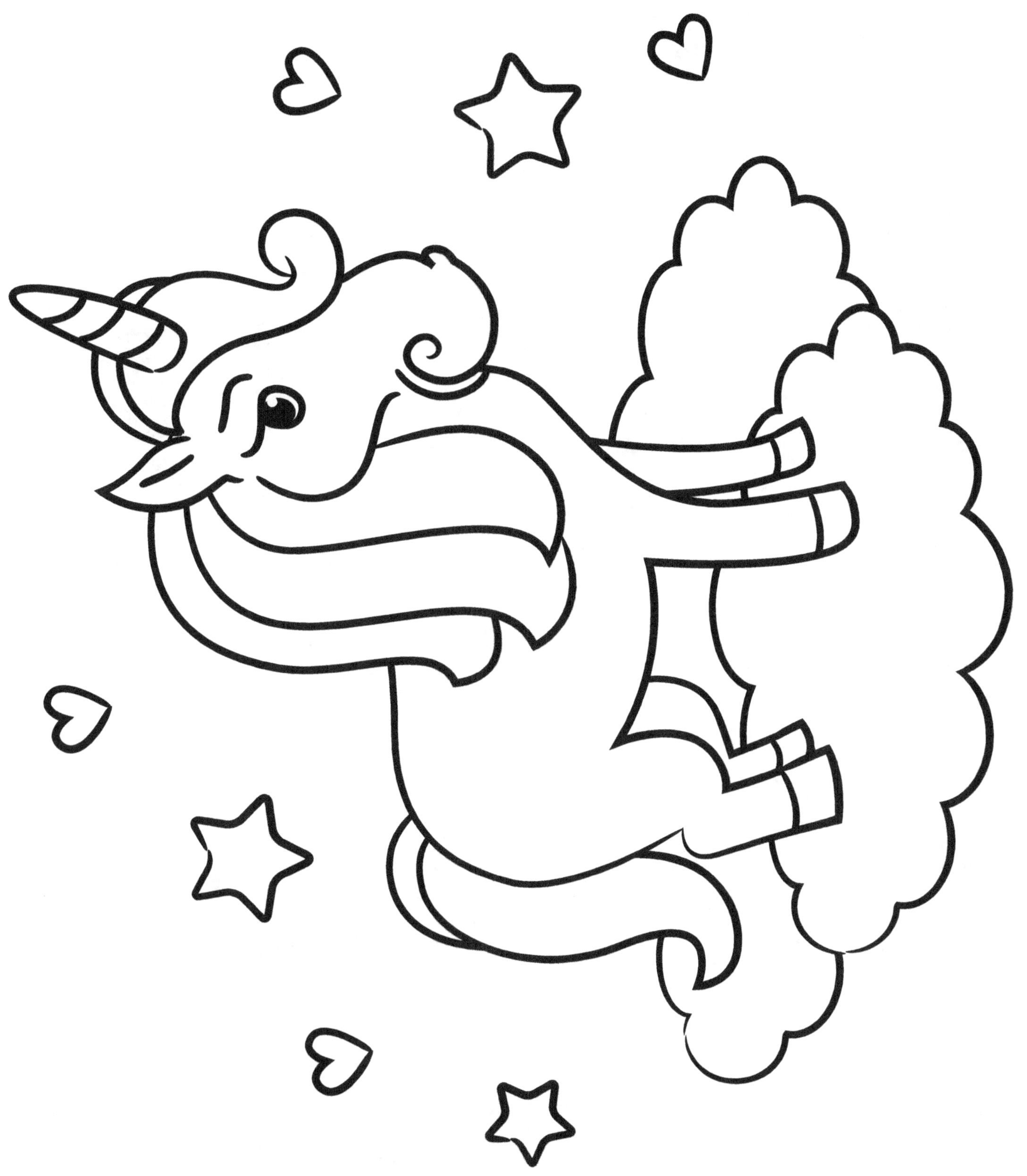

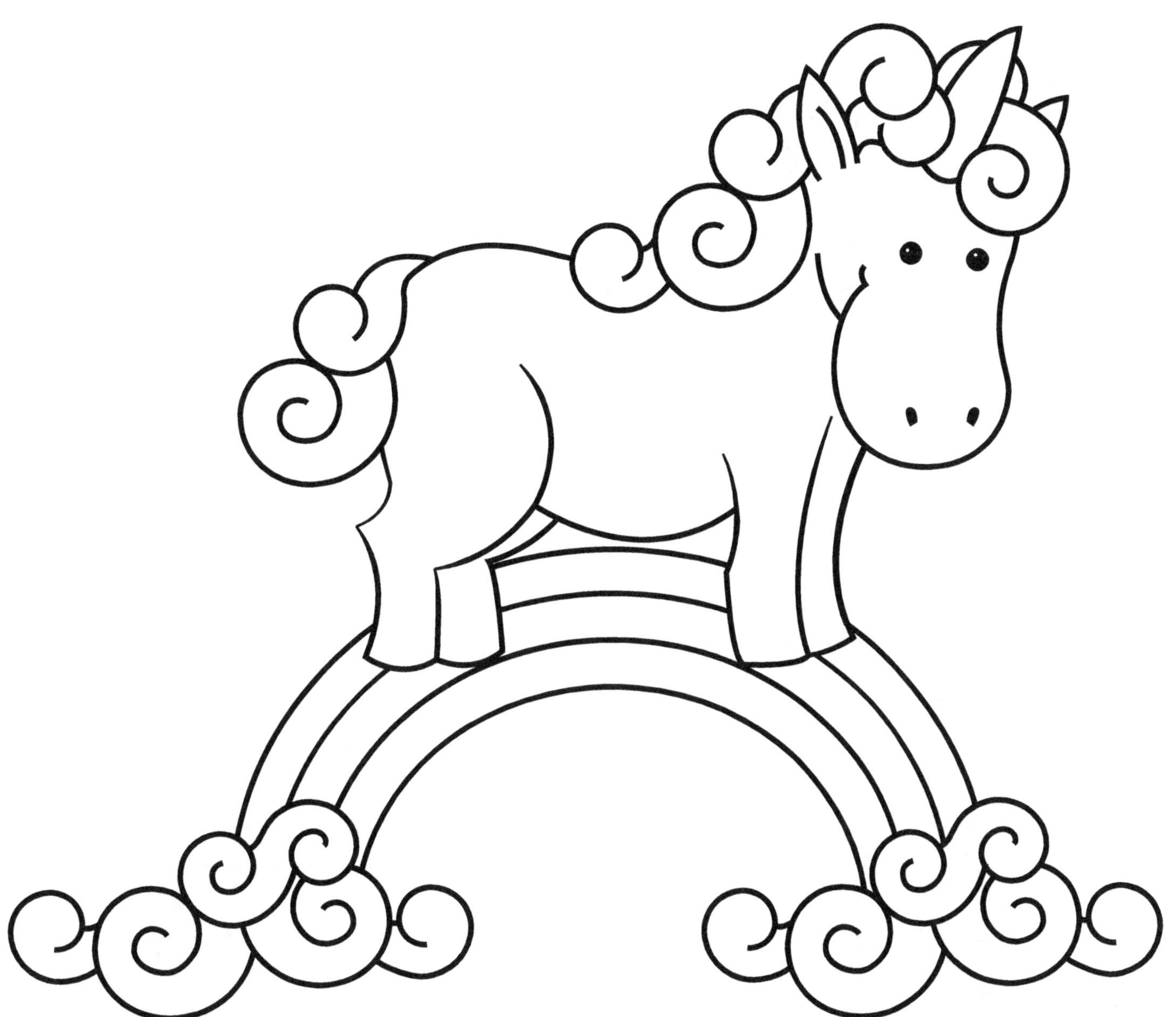

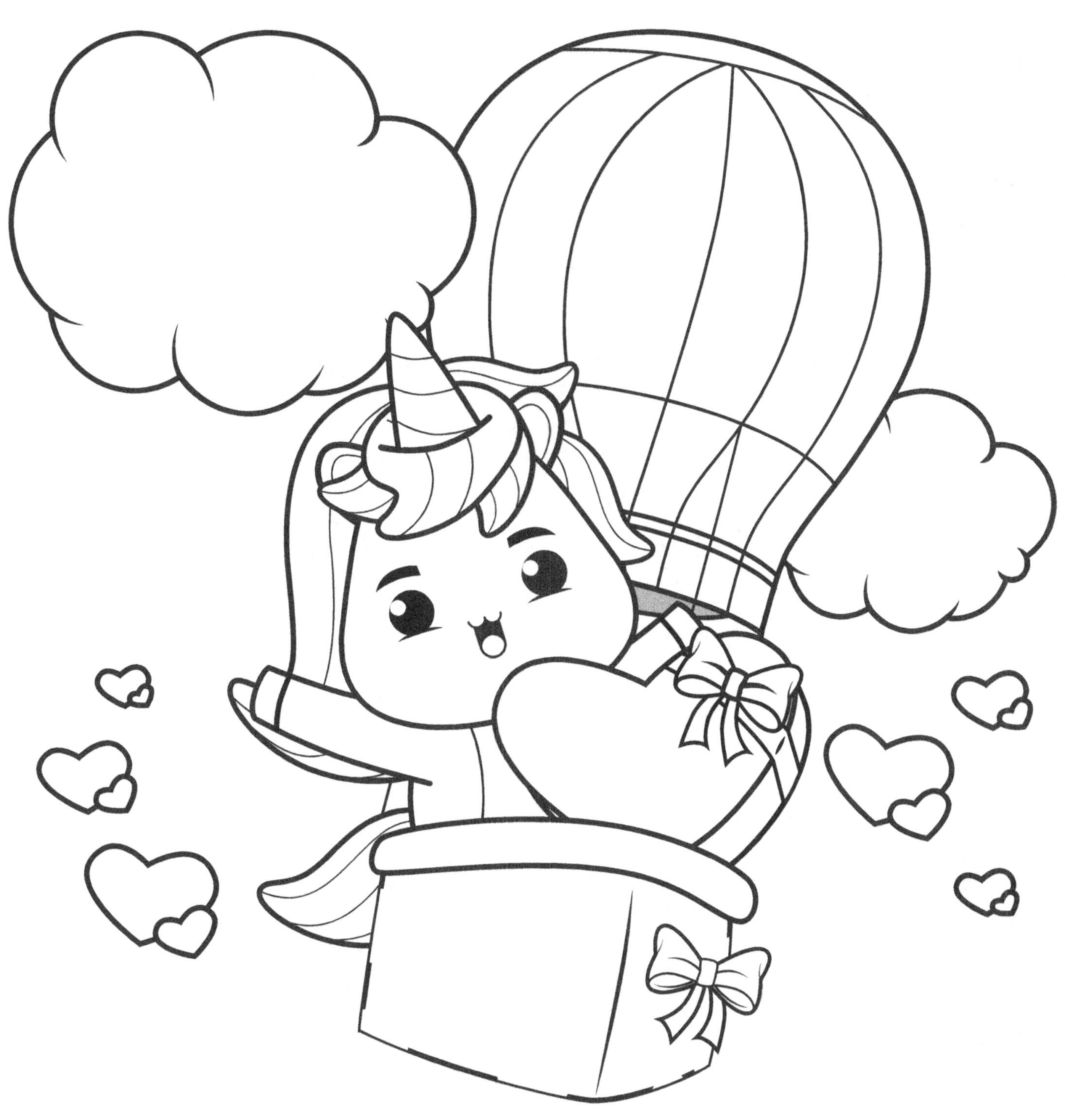

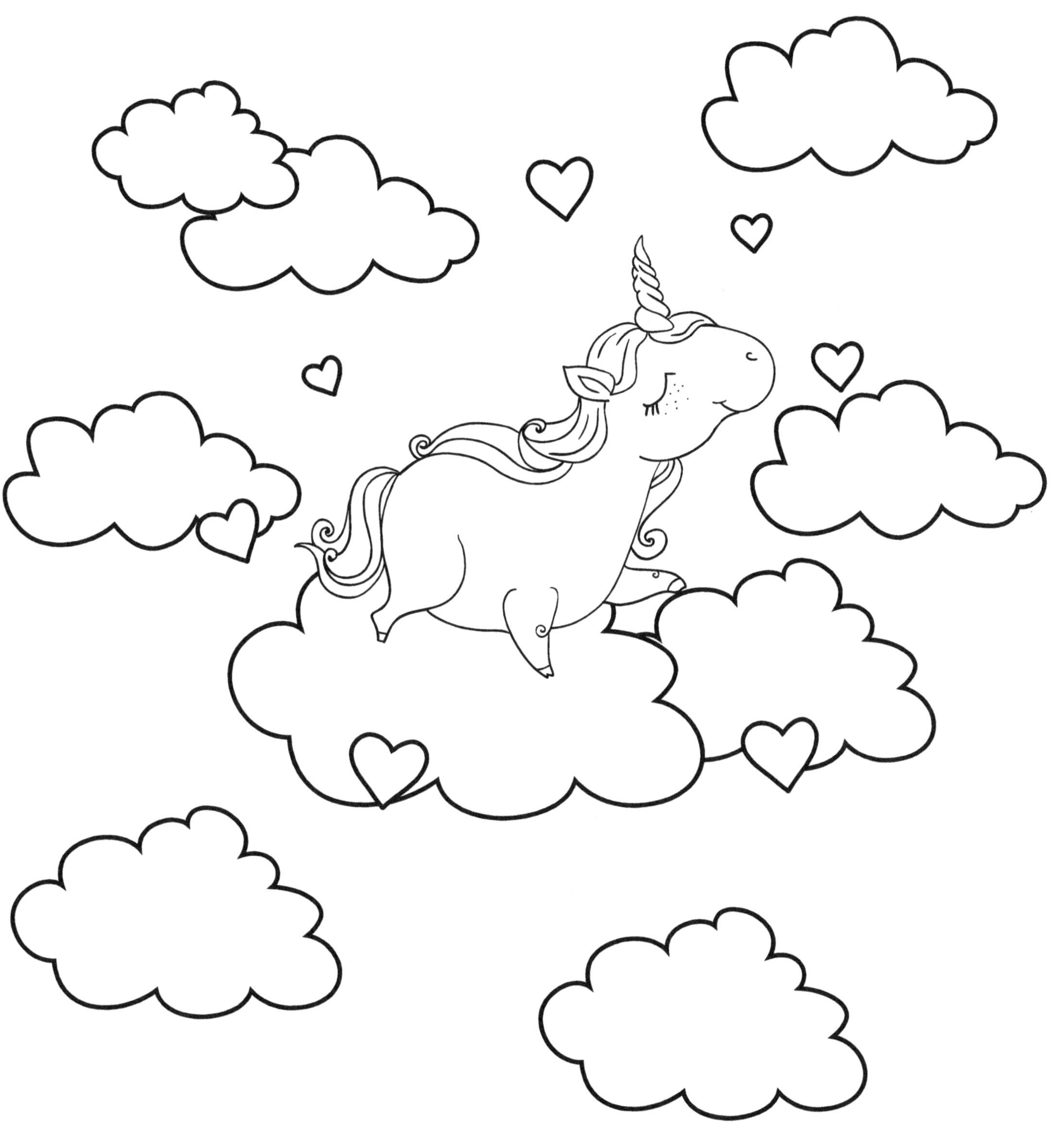

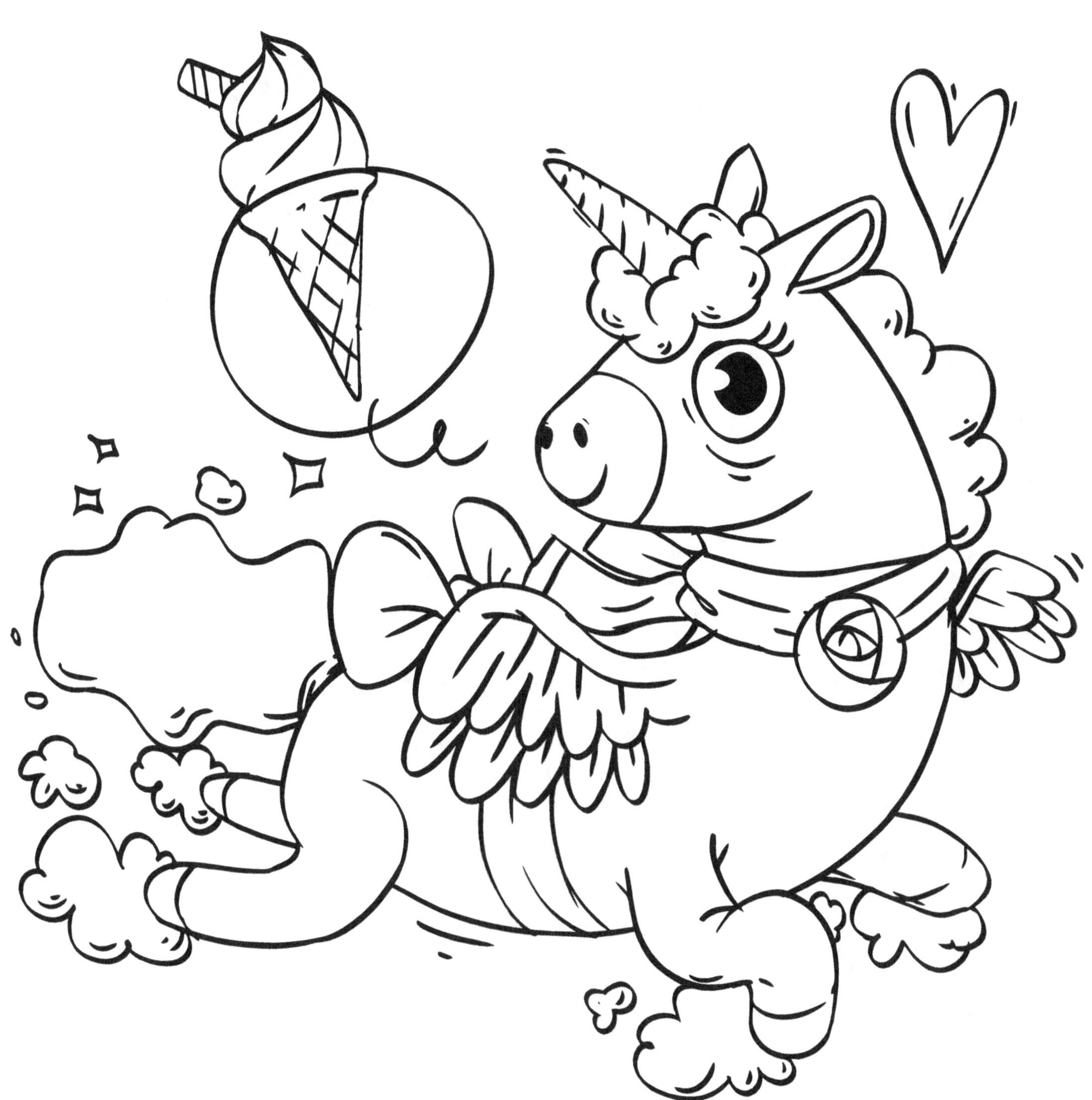

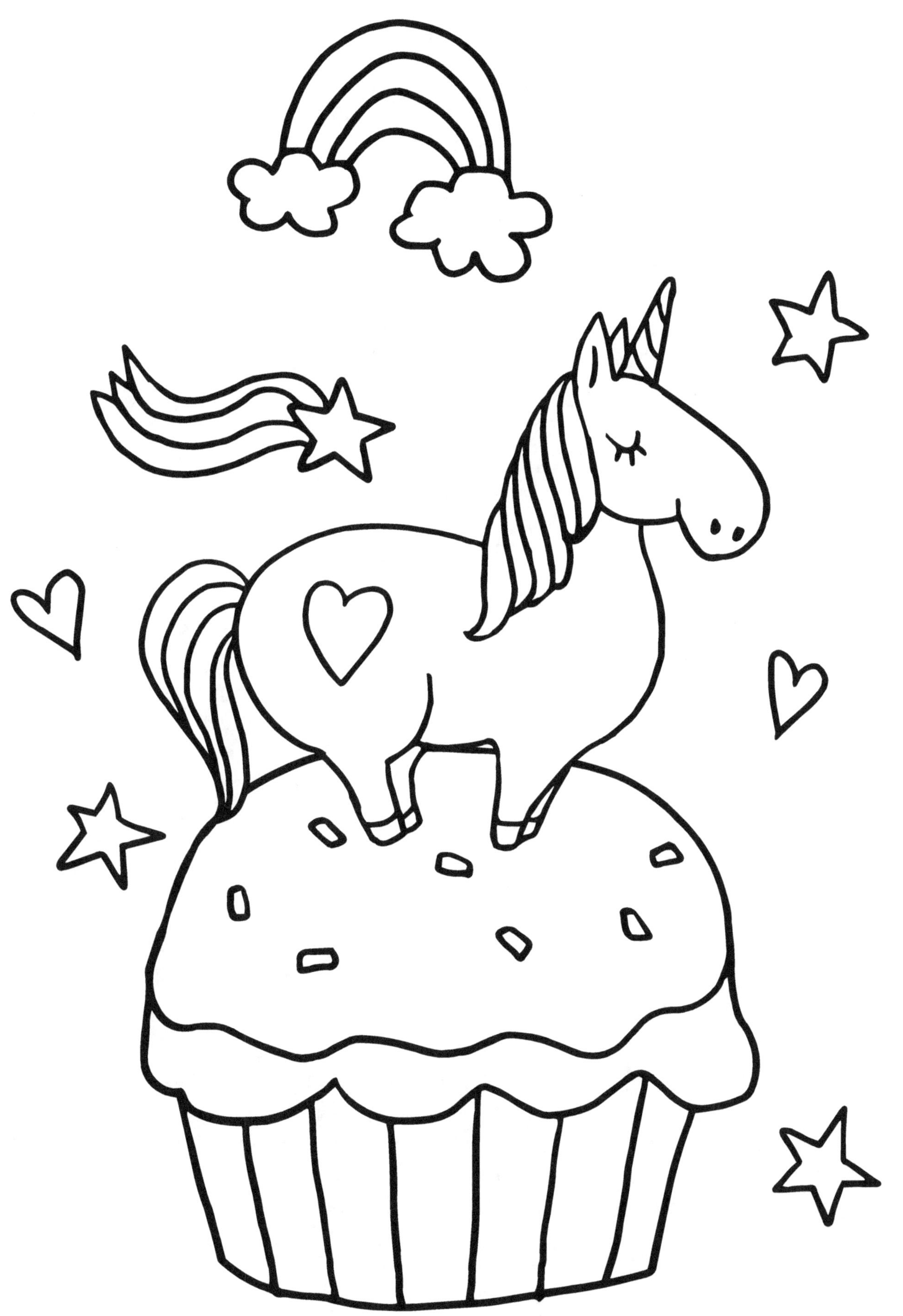

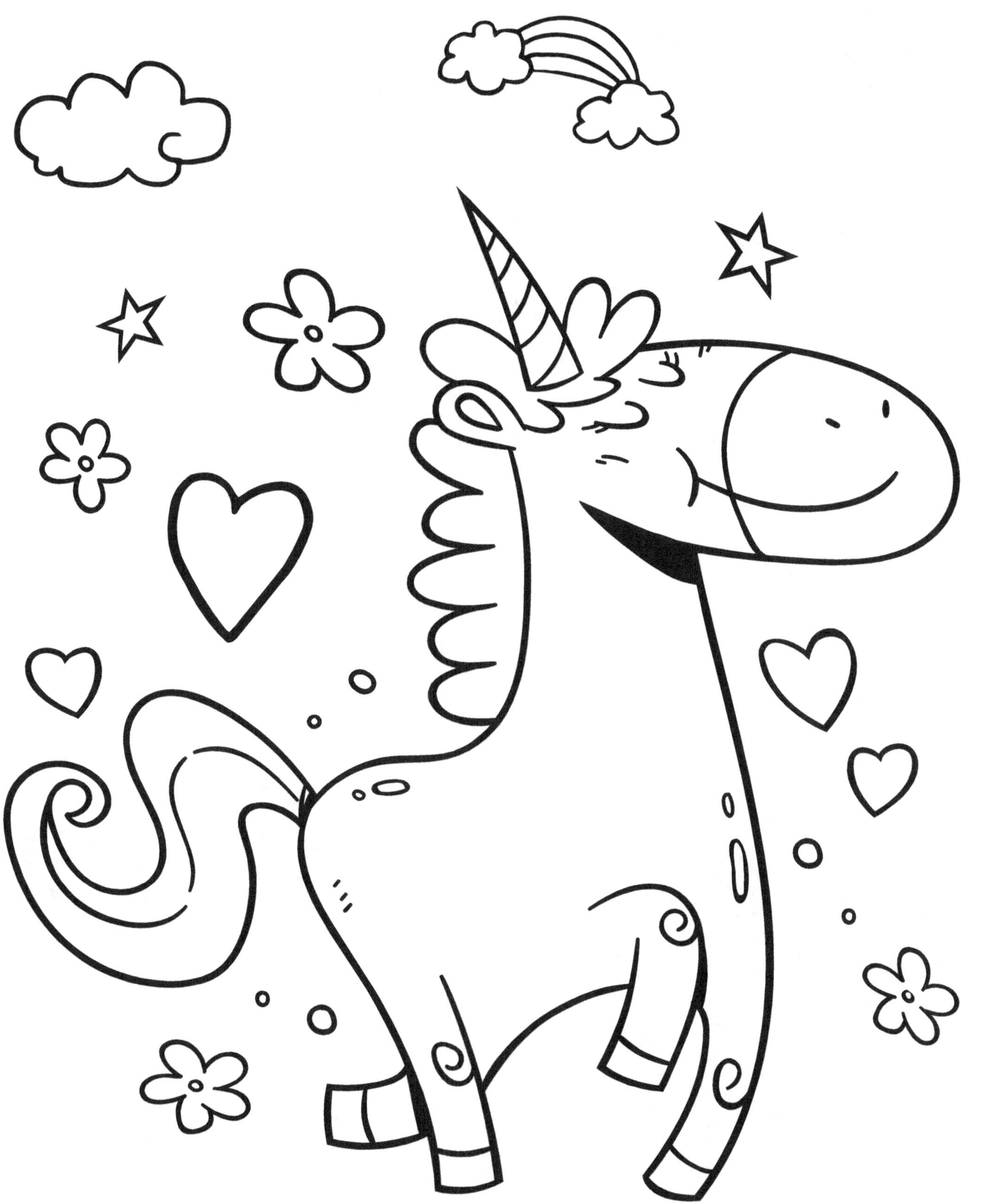

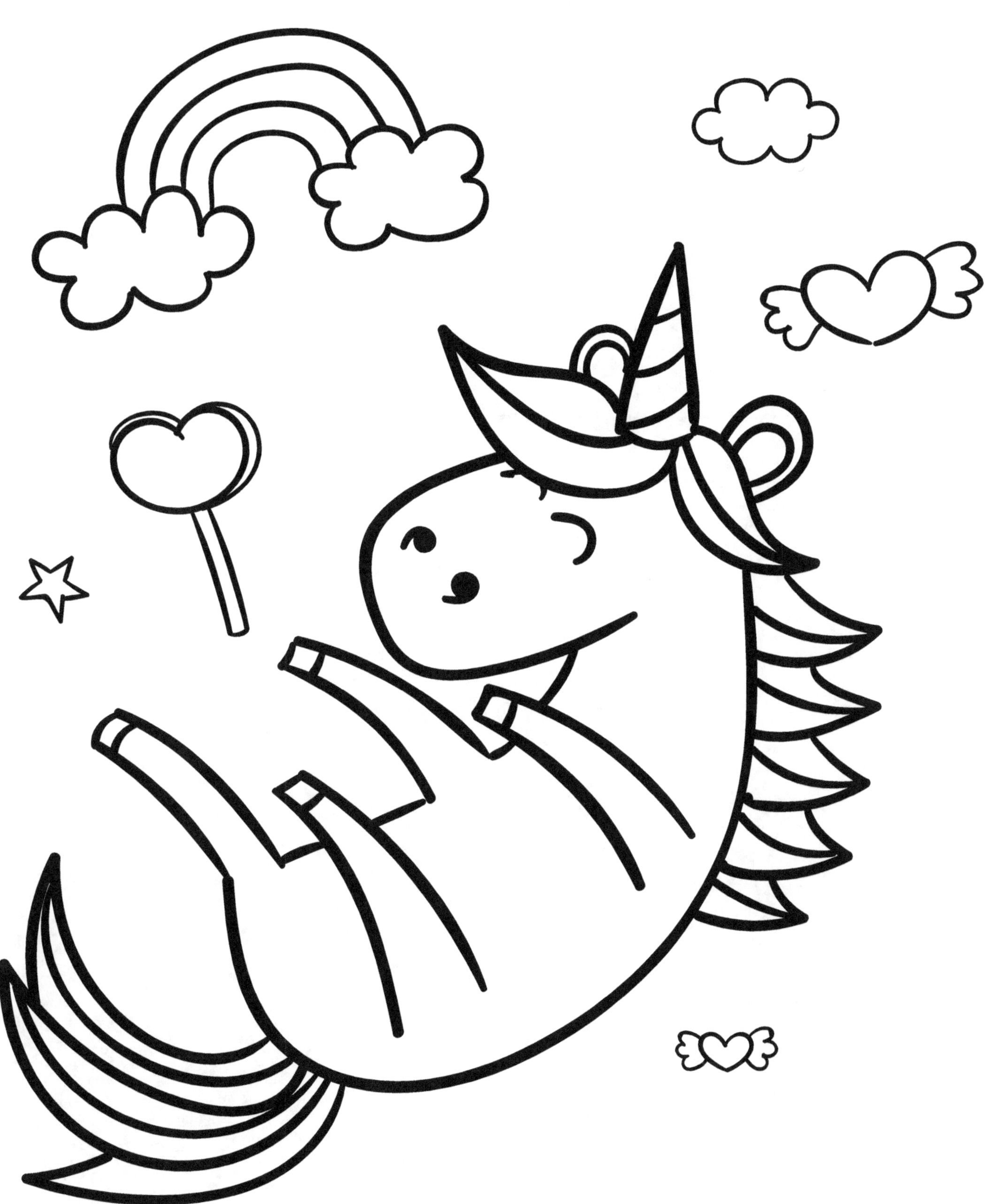

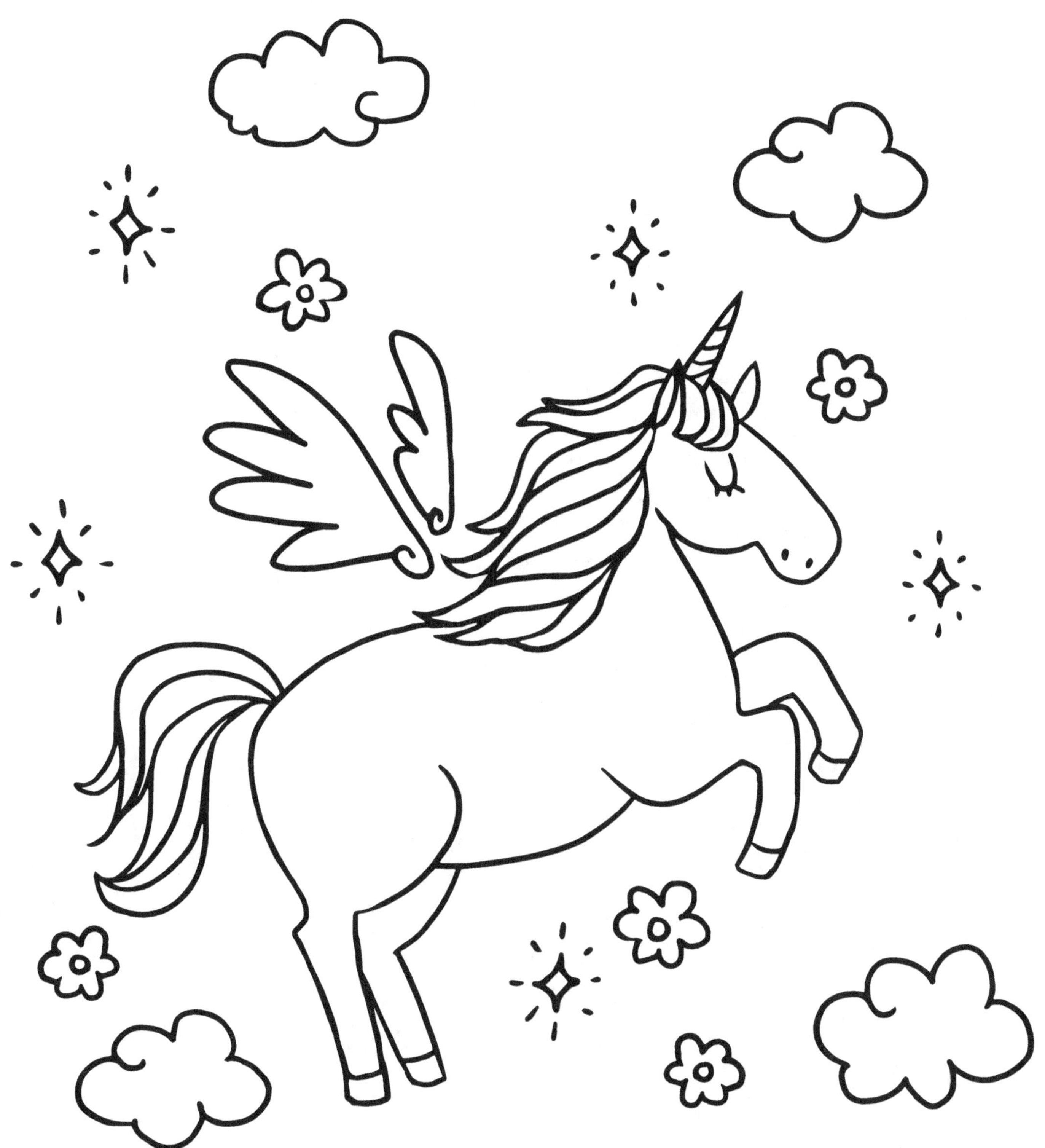

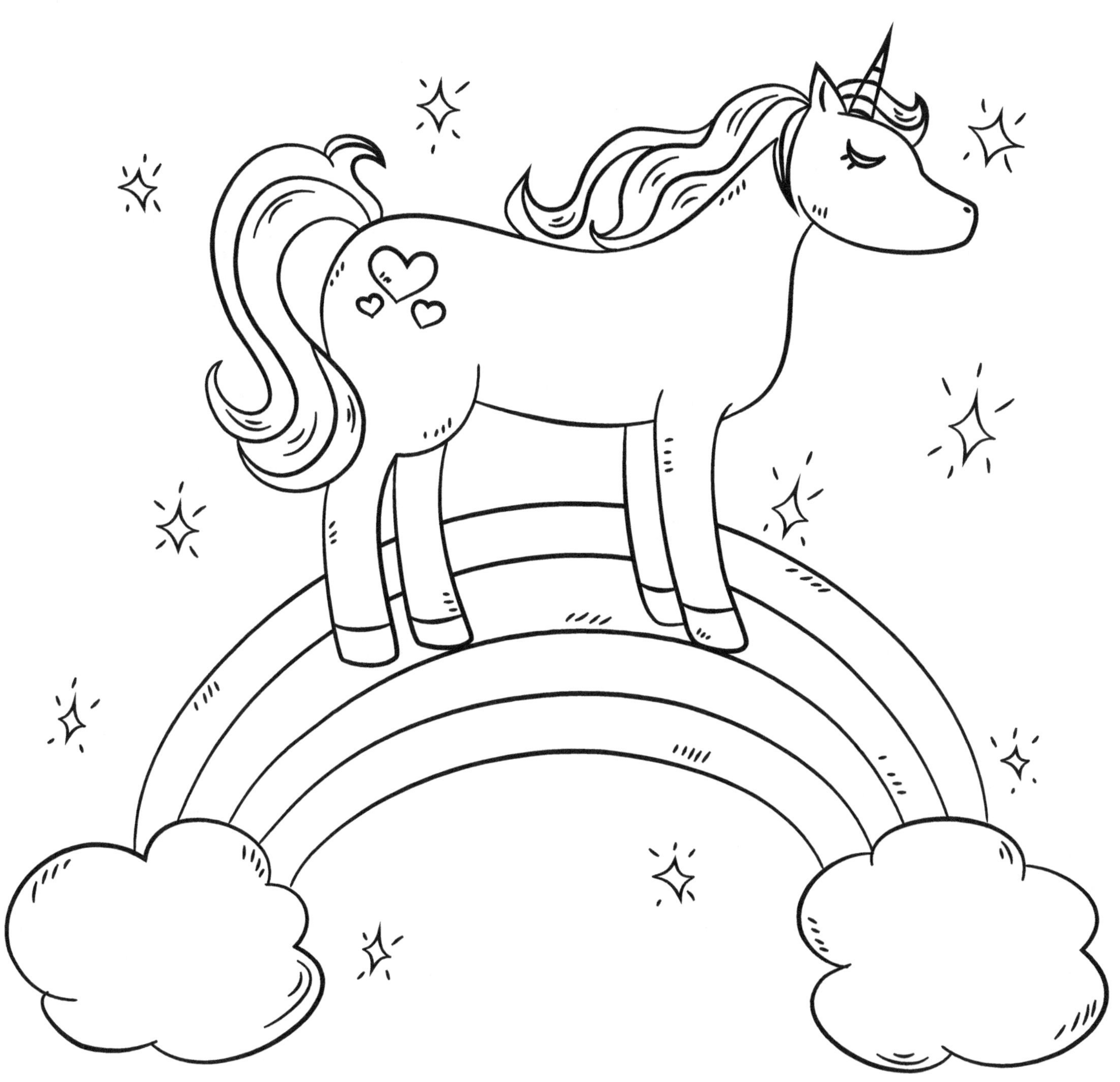

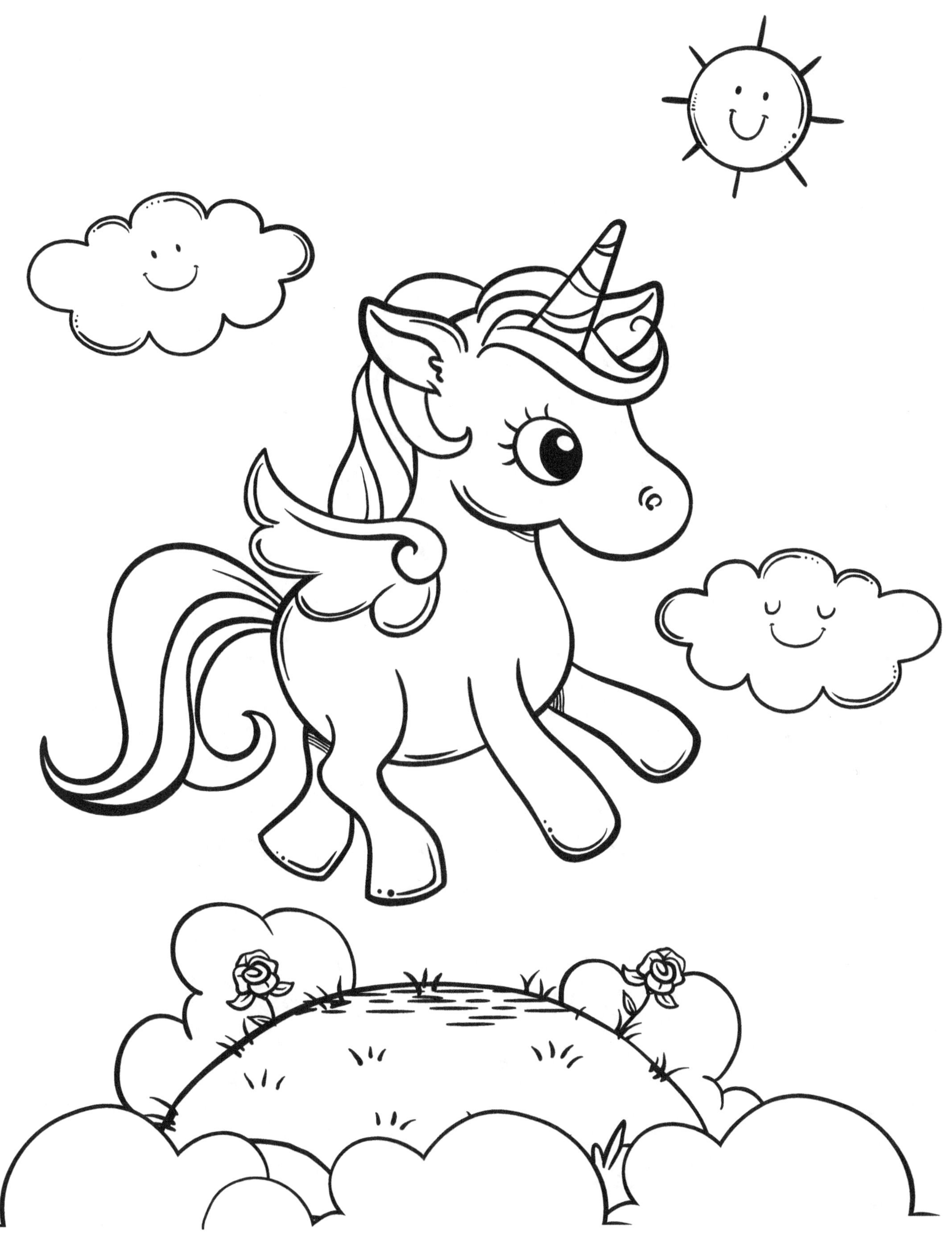

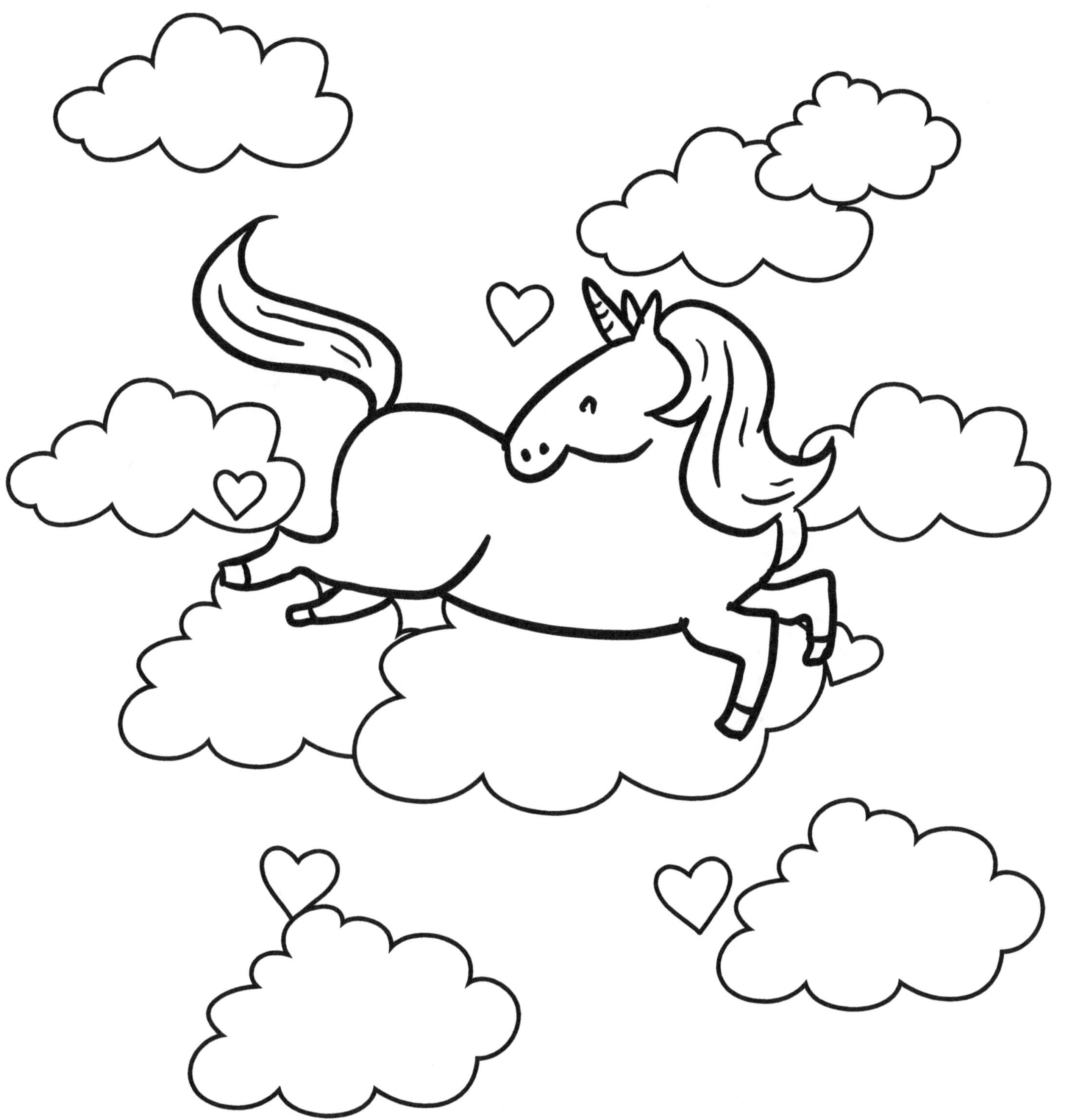

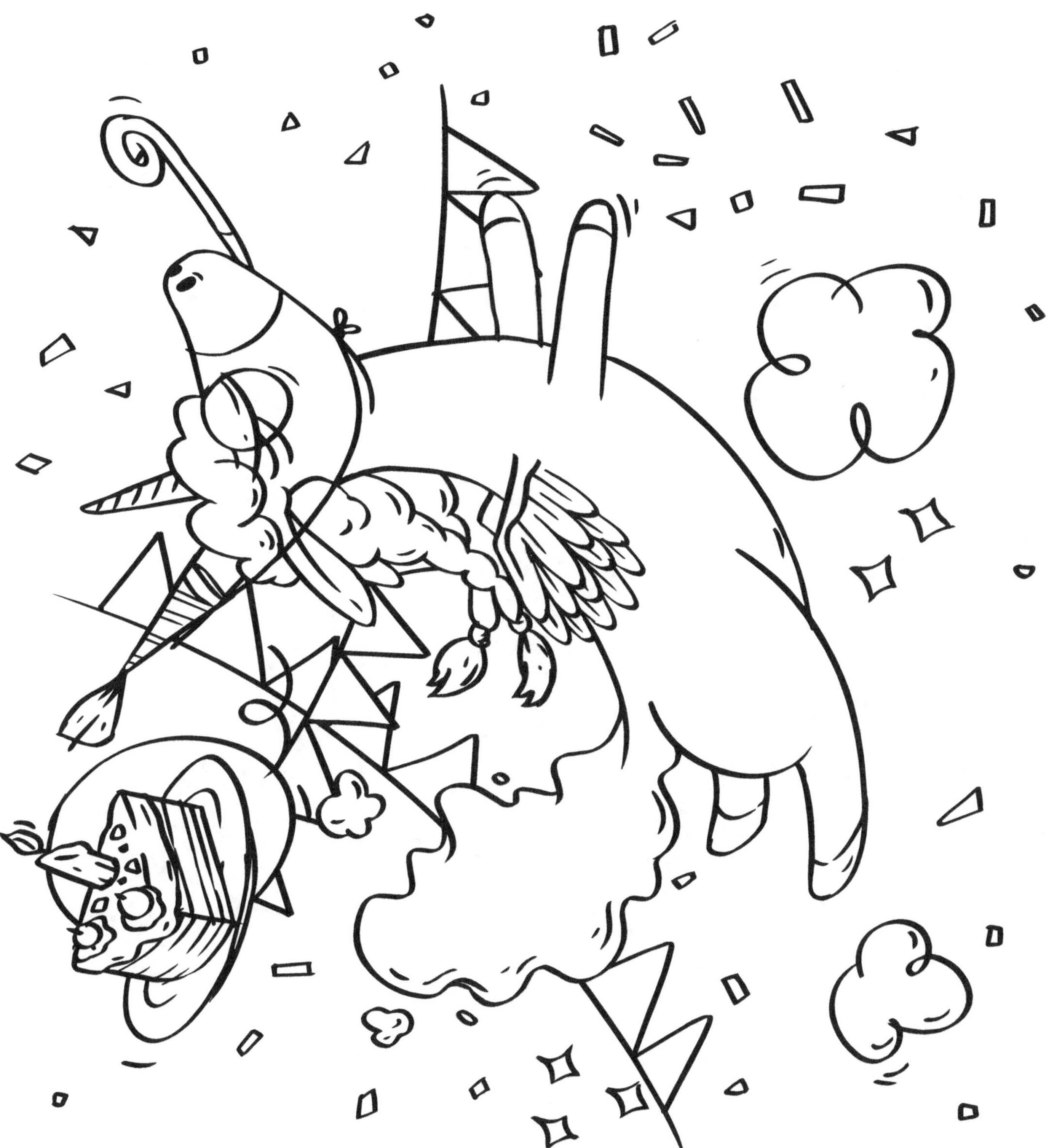

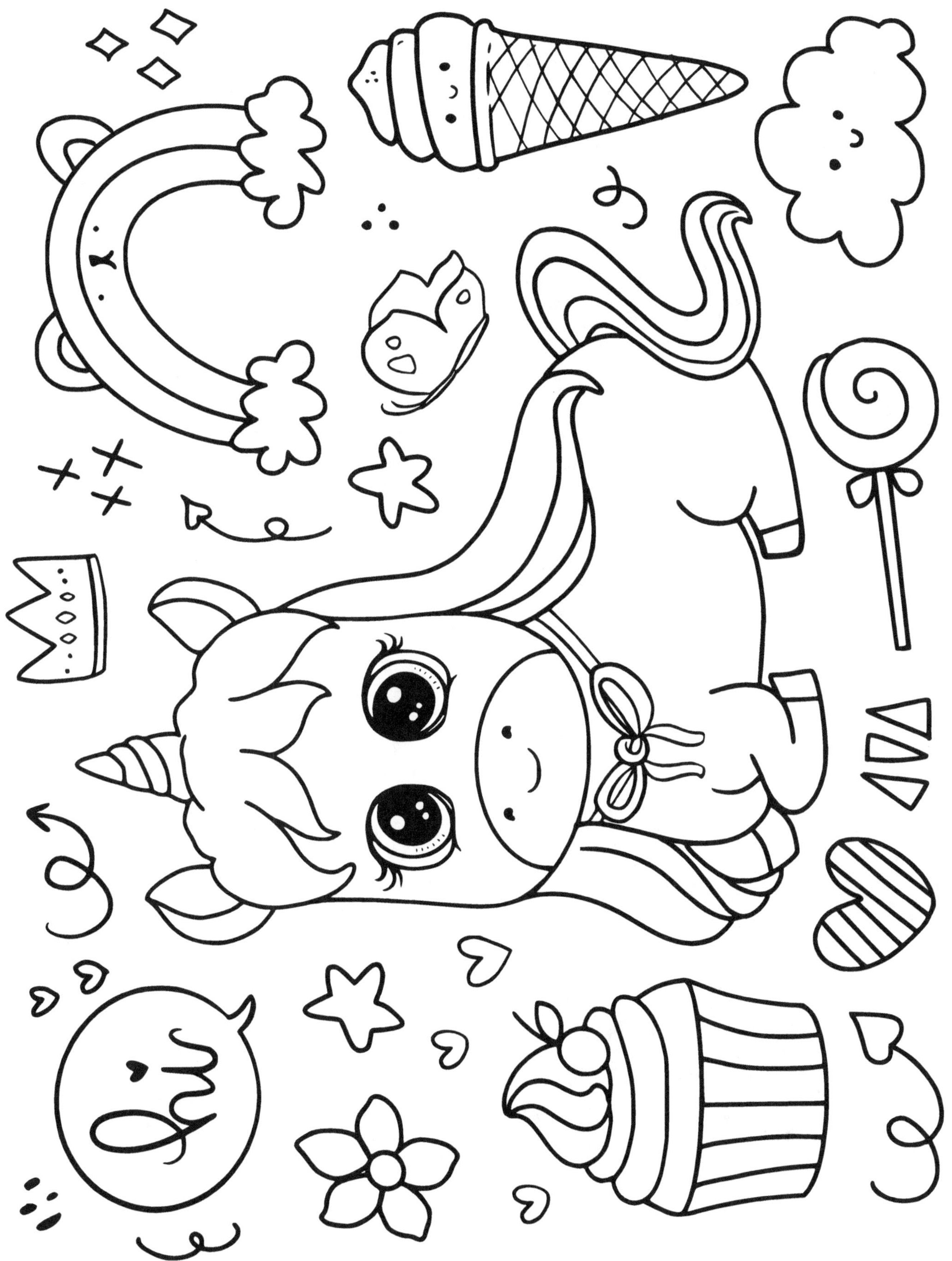

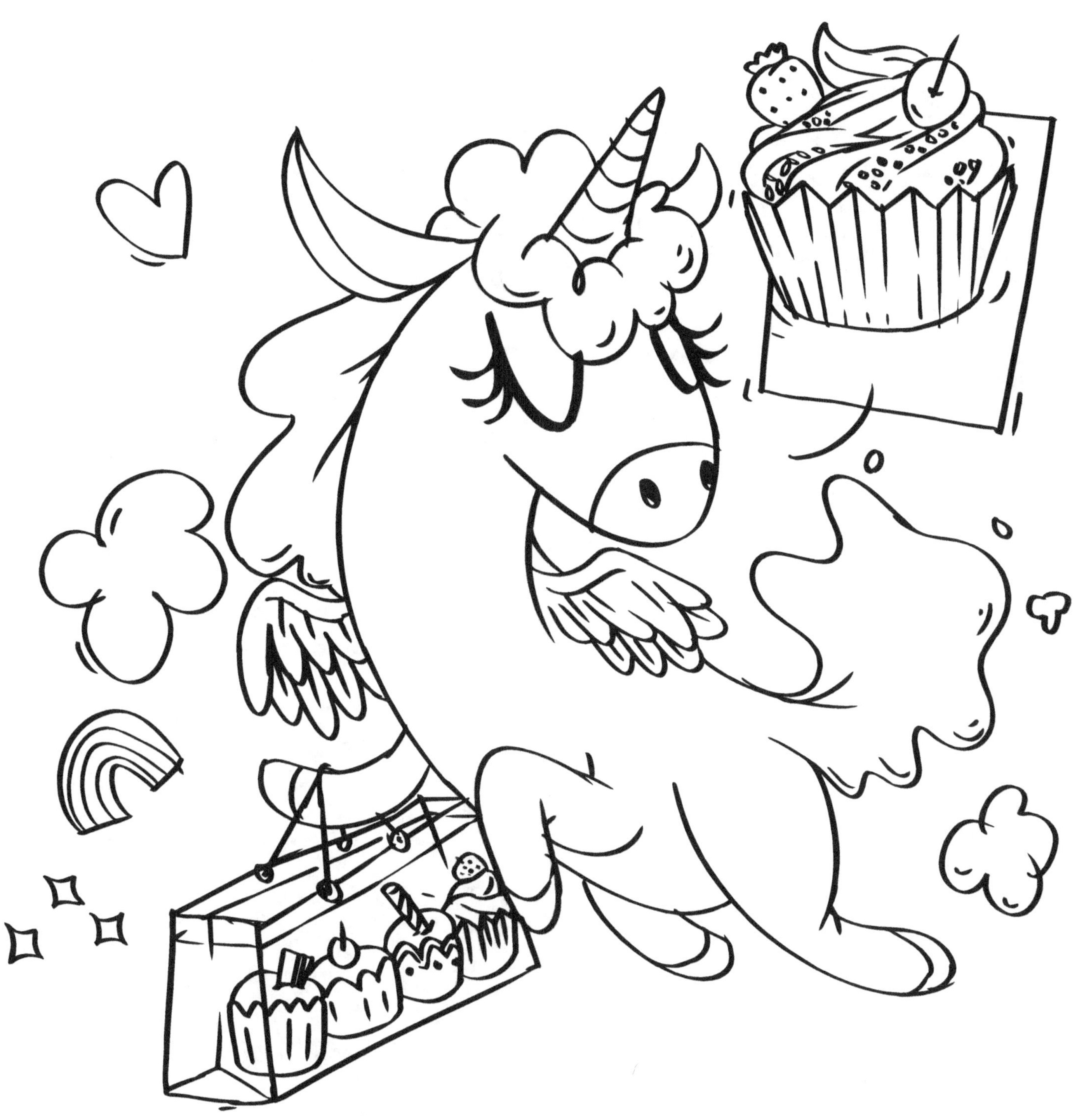

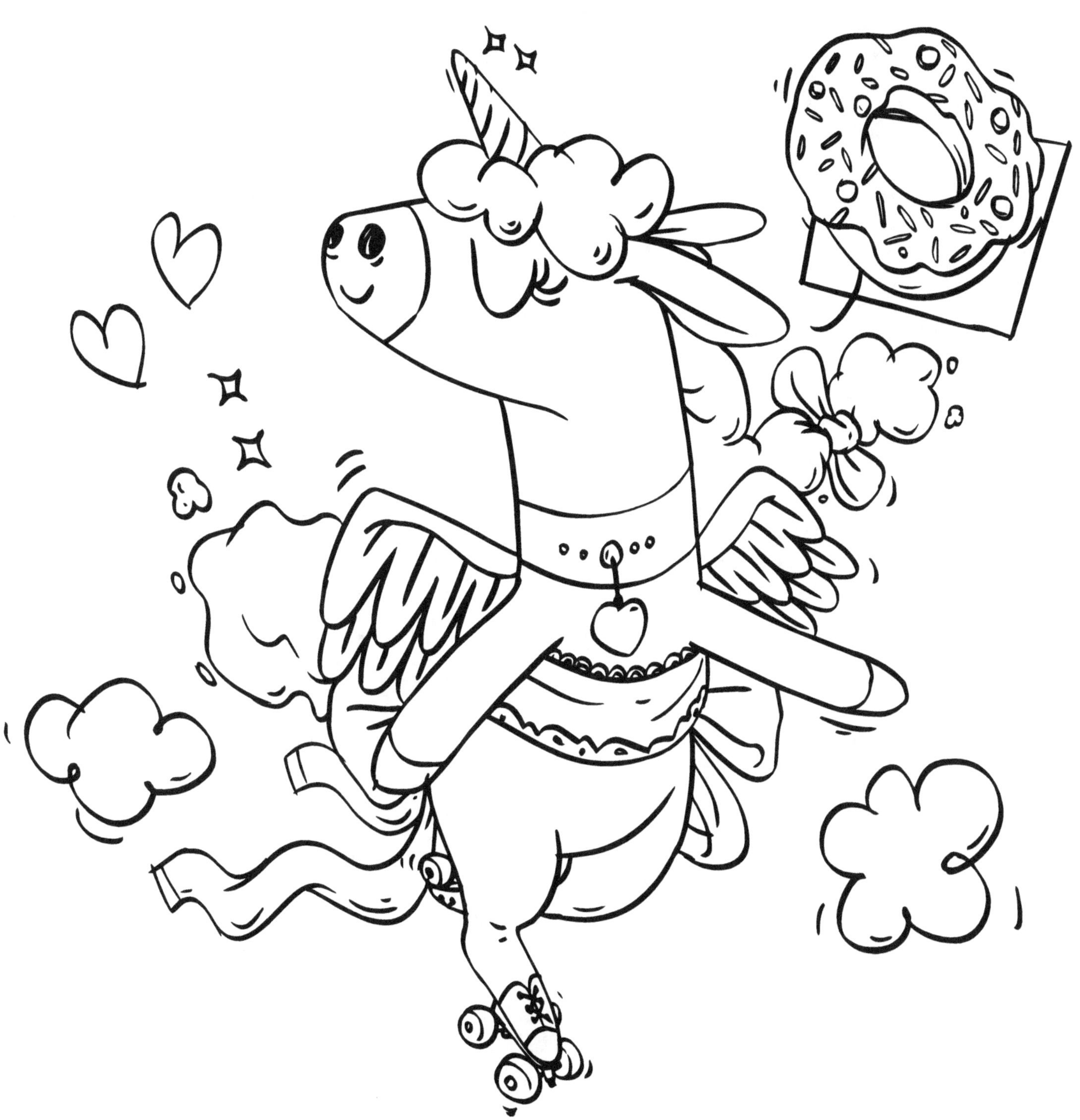

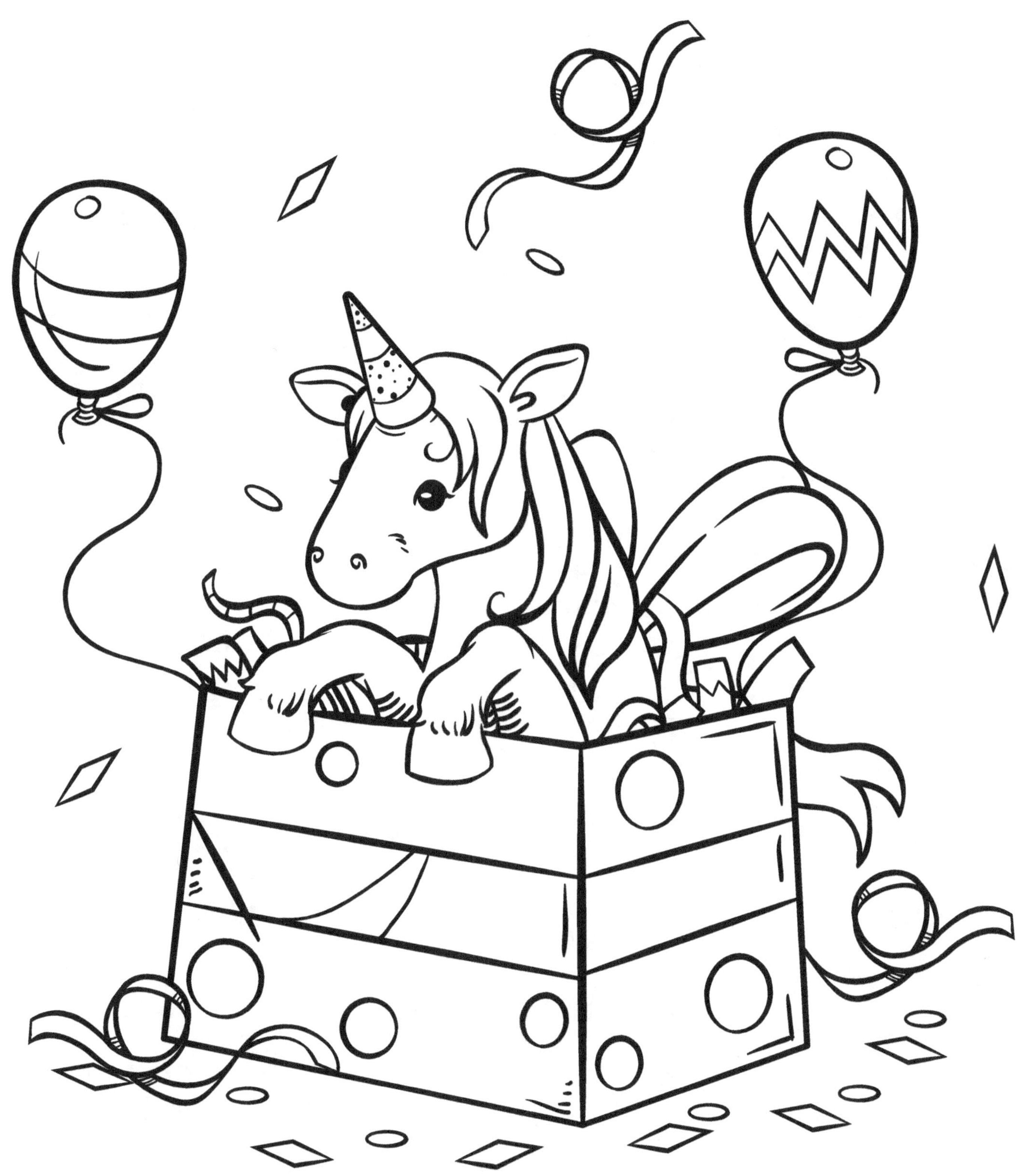

UNICORN TIME

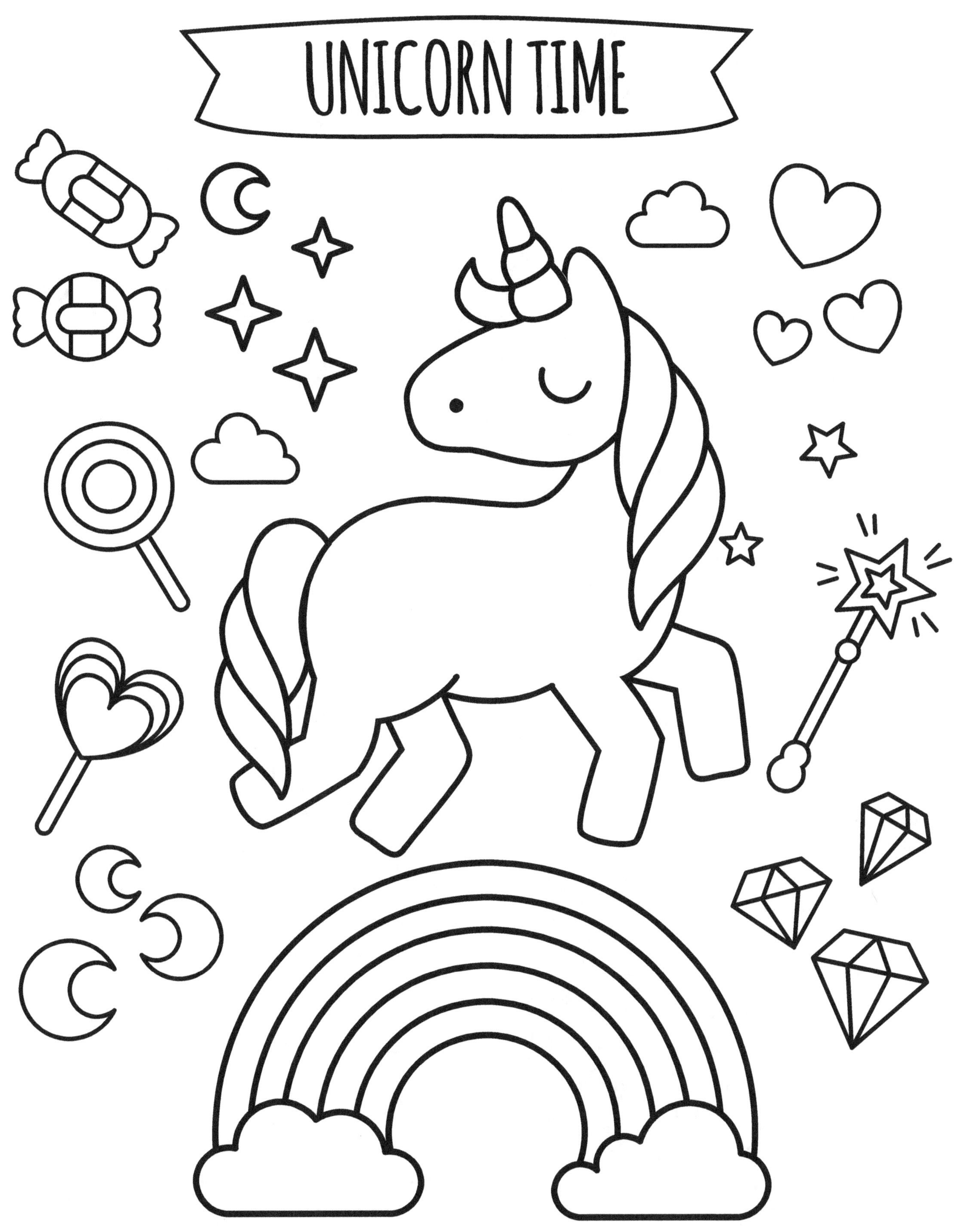

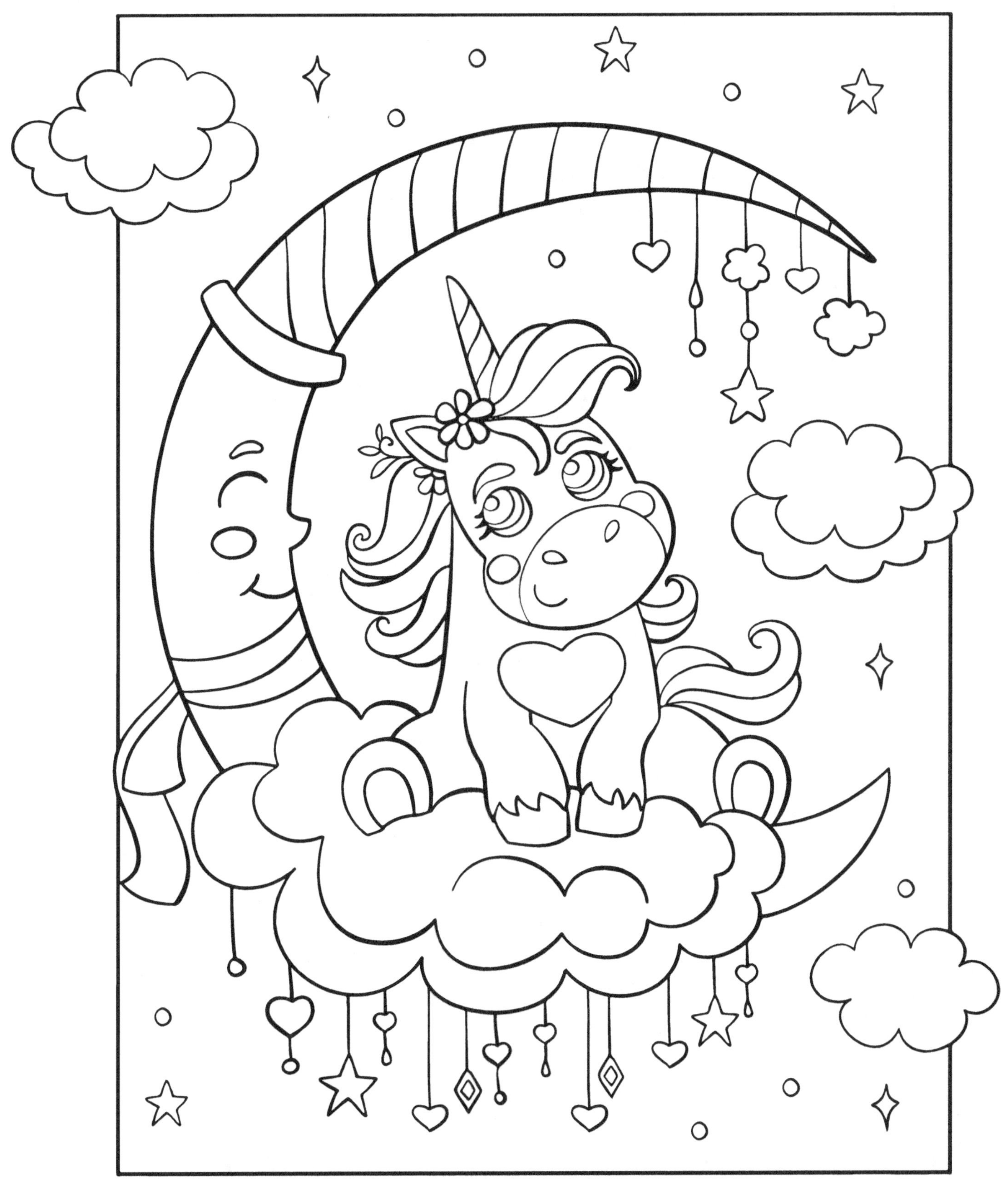

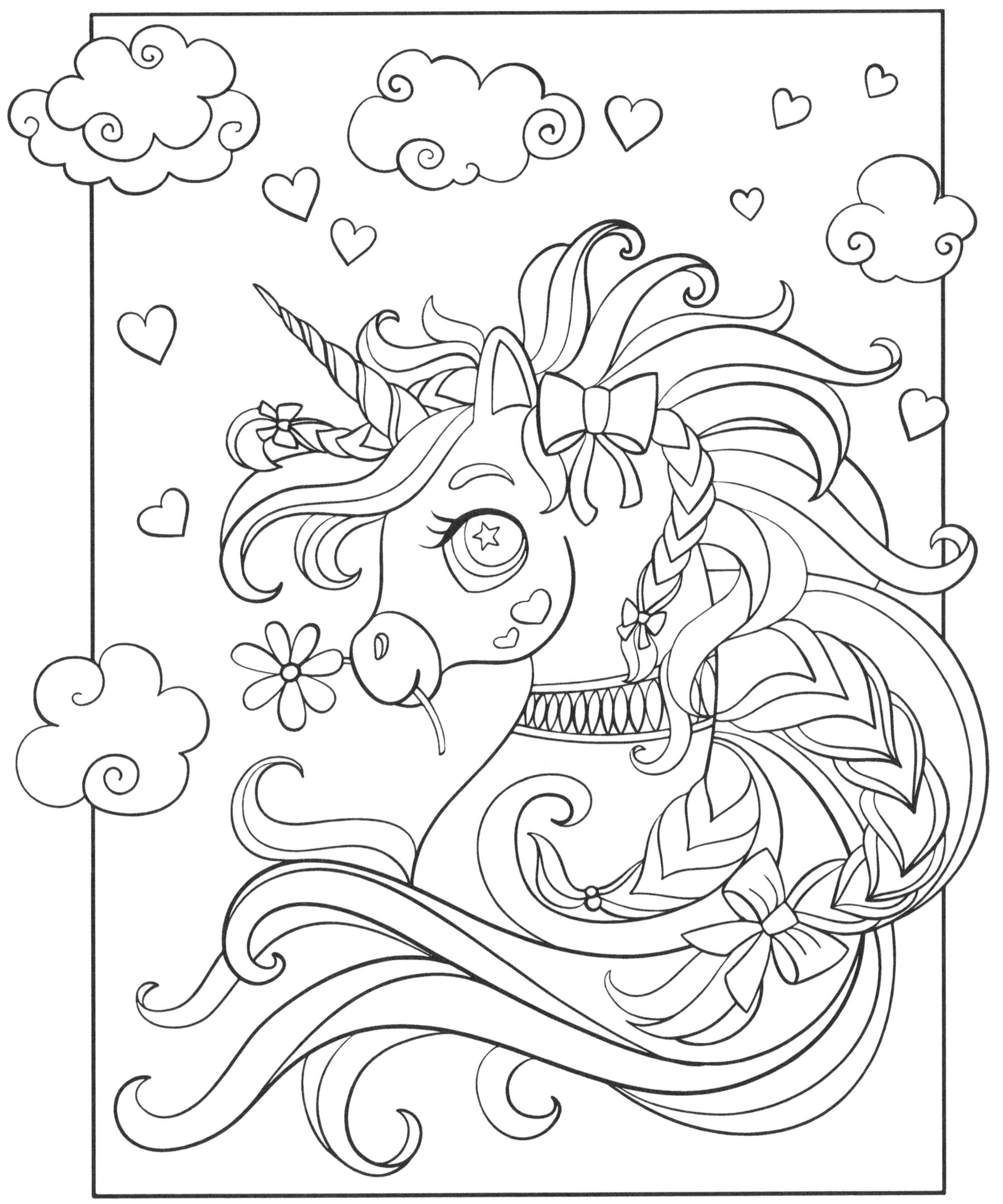

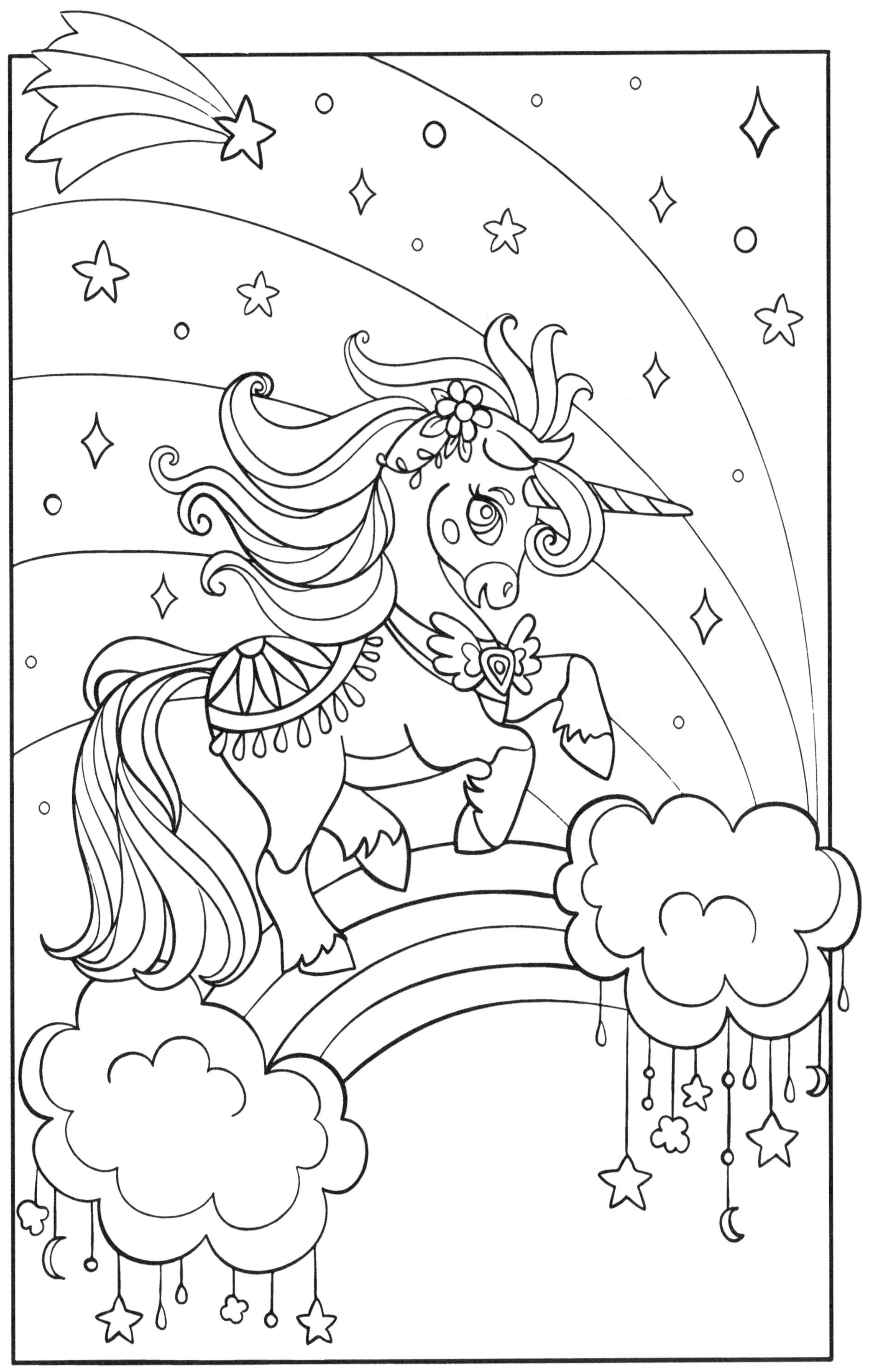

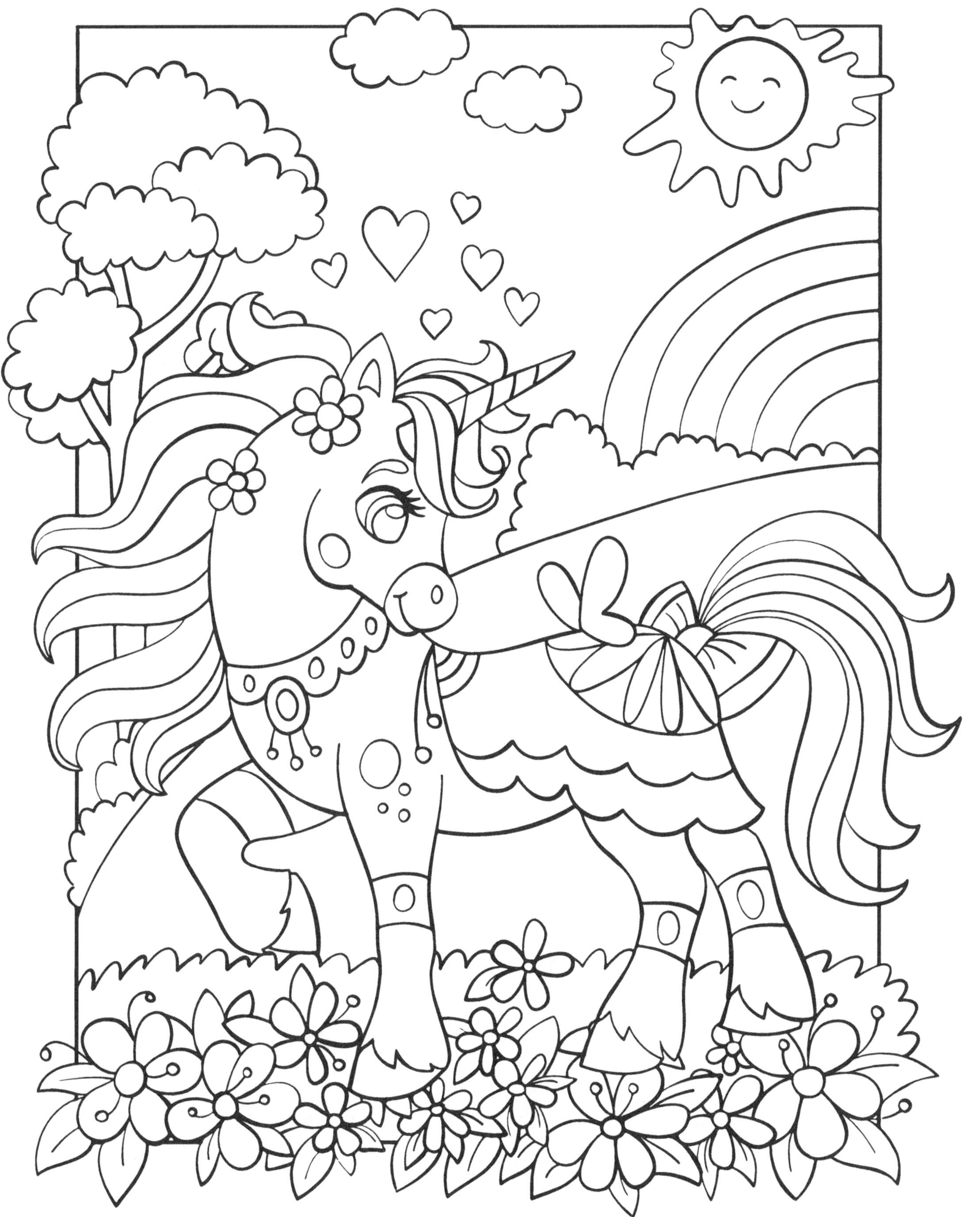

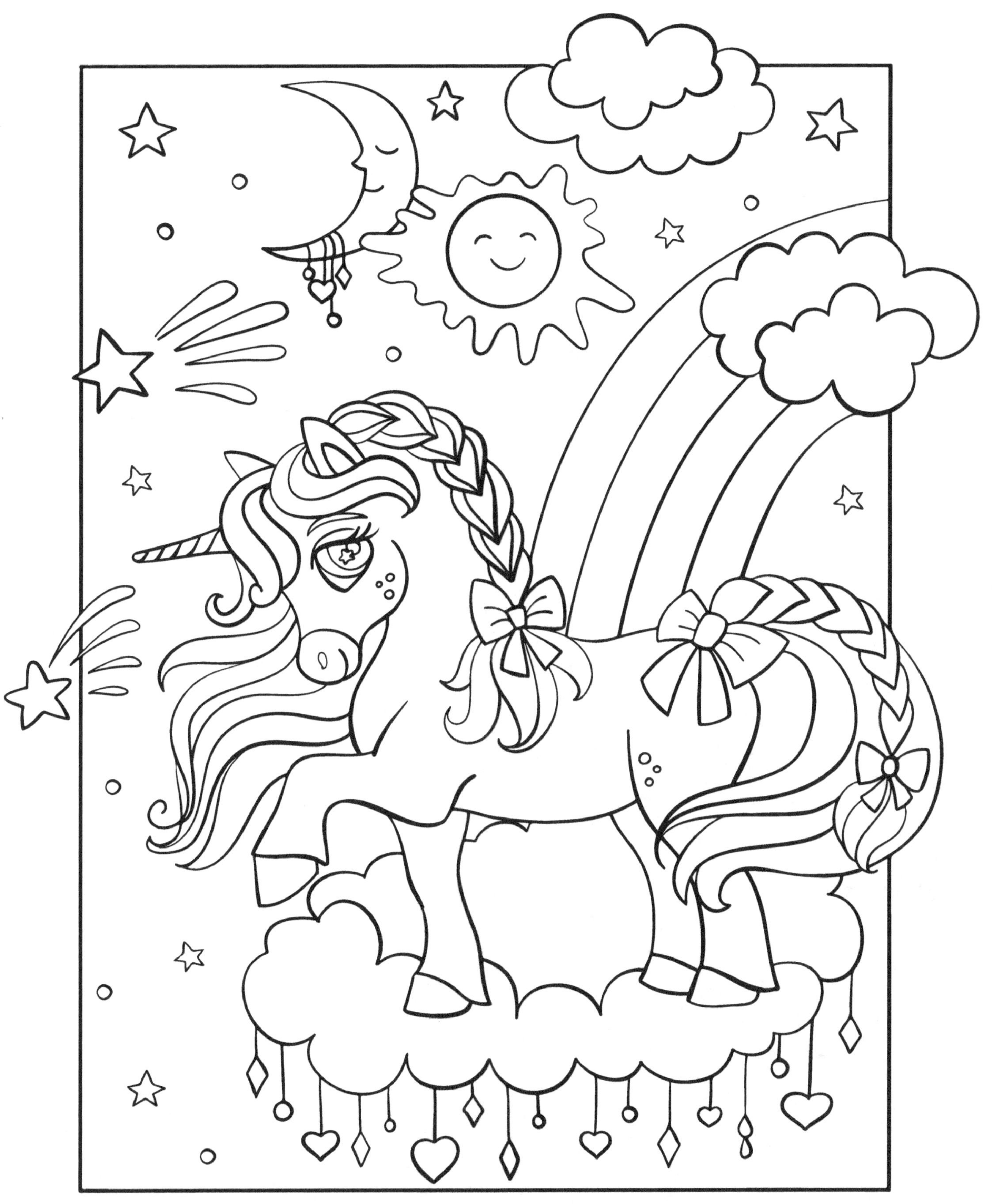

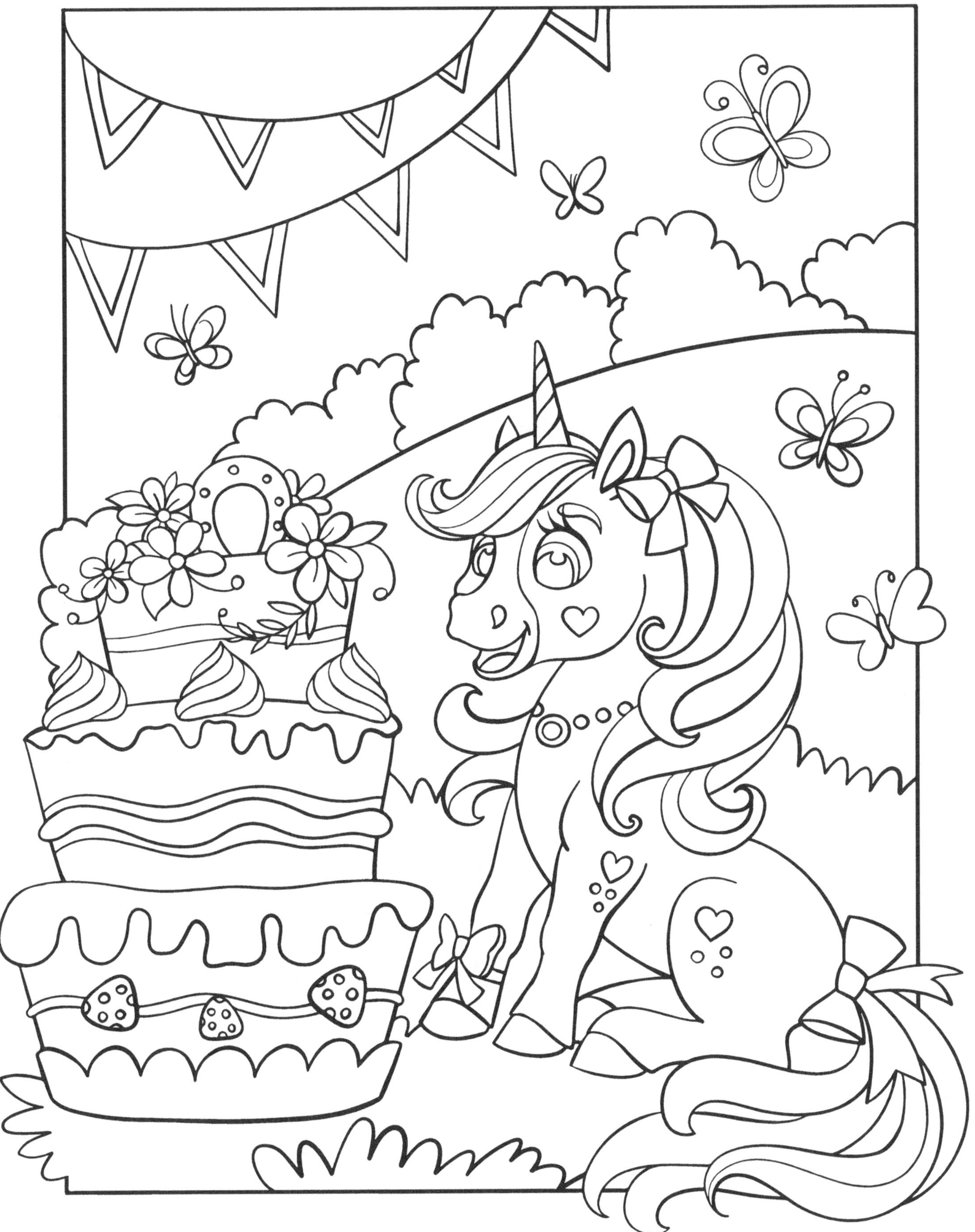

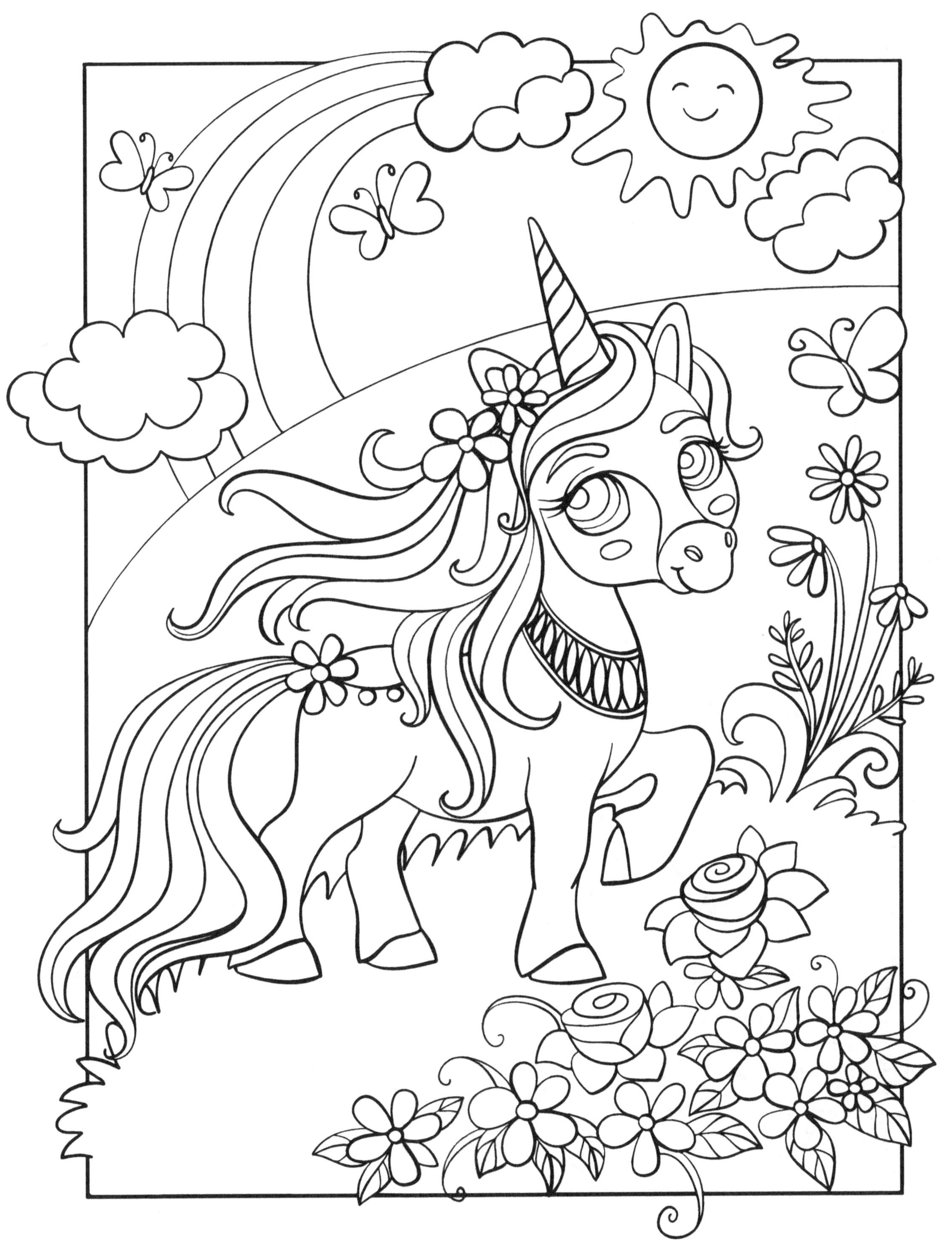

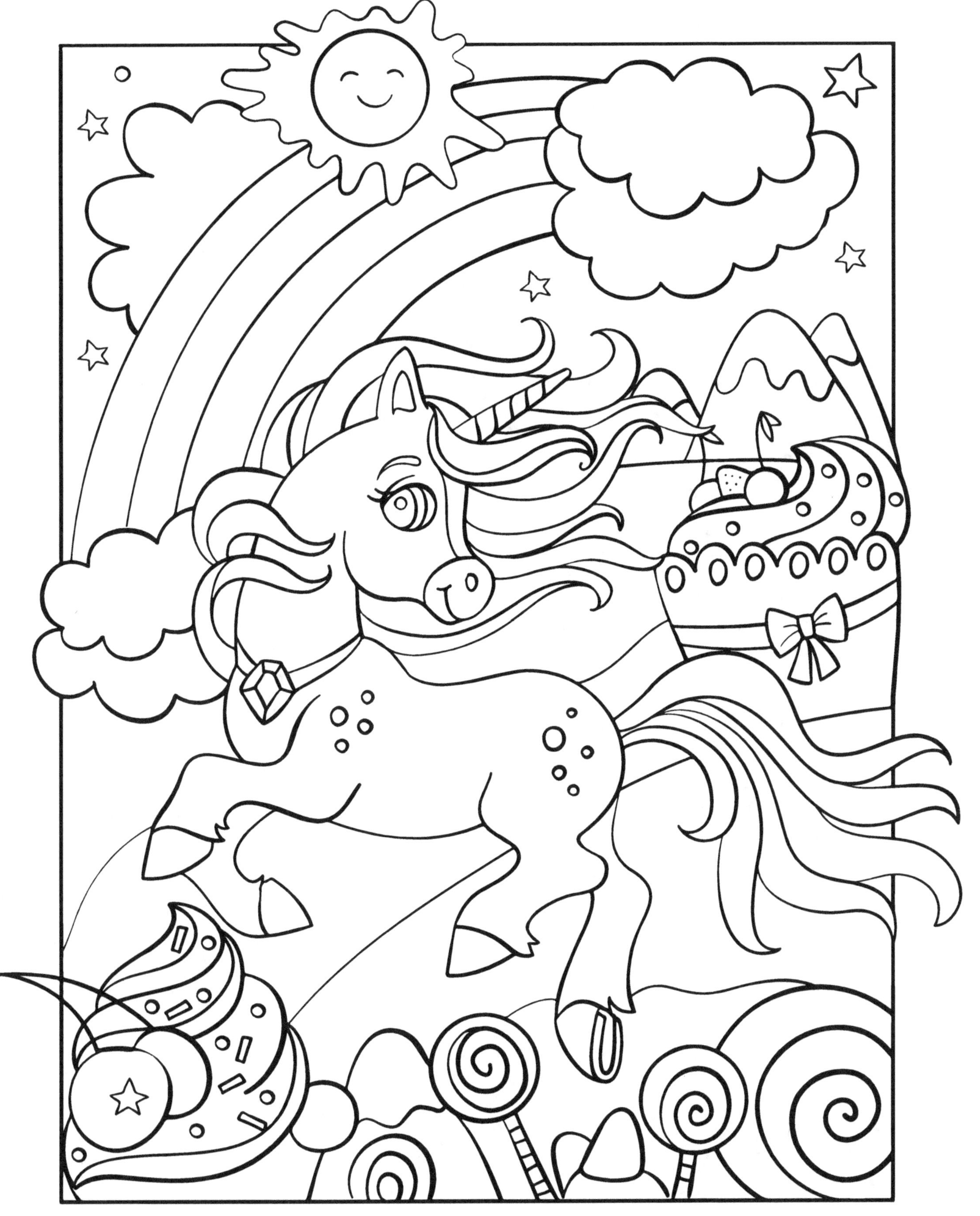

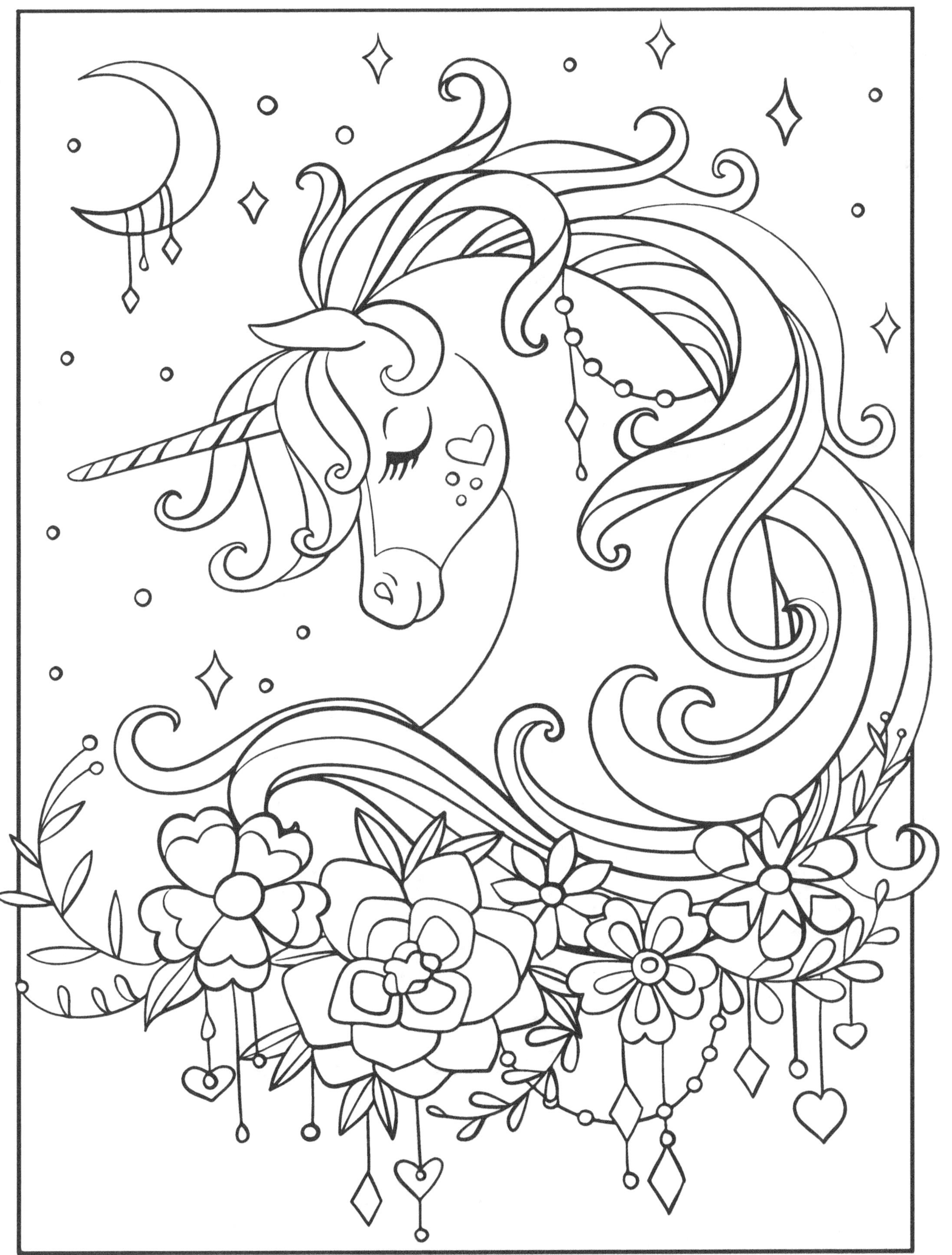

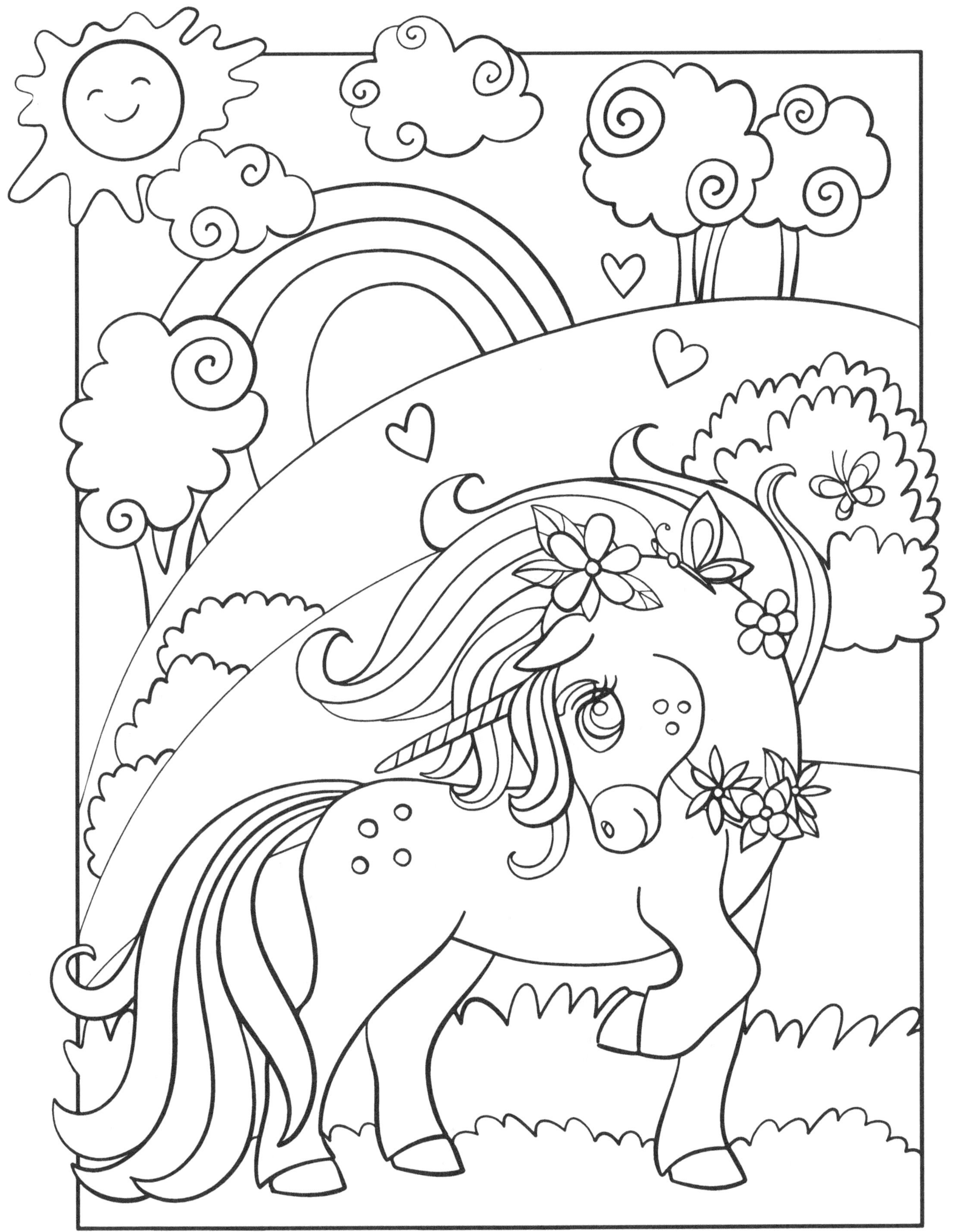

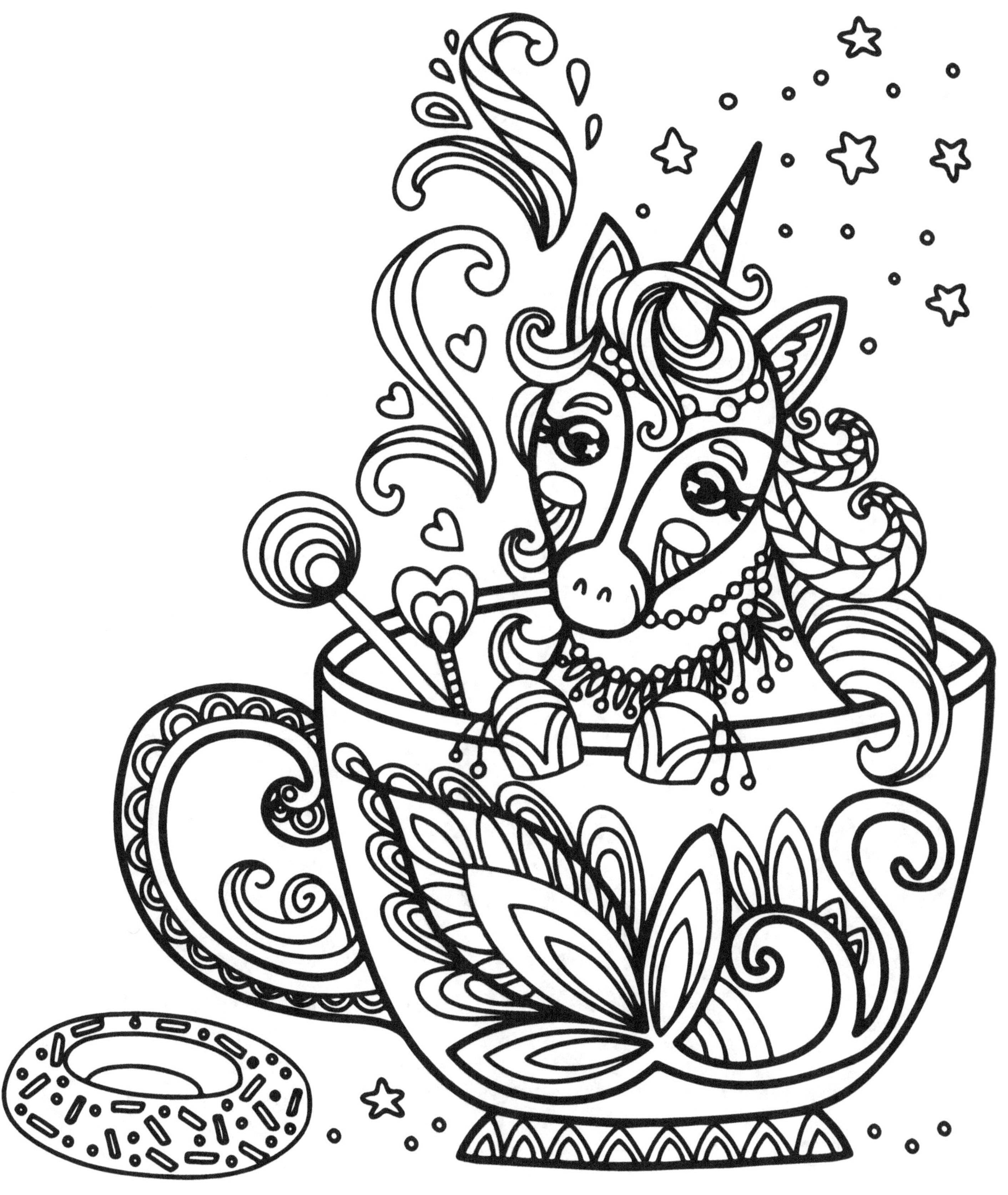

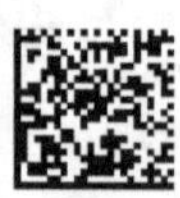

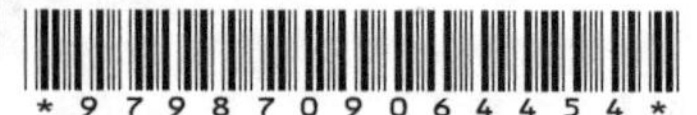